PR
GOD'S WILL

for
My Wife

LEE ROBERTS

OLIVER
NELSON

THOMAS NELSON PUBLISHERS
Nashville

To my wife,
Joann

Published in Nashville, Tennessee, by Oliver-Nelson Books, a division of Thomas Nelson, Inc., Publishers, and distributed in Canada by Lawson Falle, Ltd., Cambridge, Ontario.

The Bible version used in this publication is THE NEW KING JAMES VERSION. Copyright © 1979, 1980, 1982, Thomas Nelson, Inc., Publishers. Verses have been modified to fit the prayer format.

Printed in the United States of America.

ISBN 0-8407-9177-1

Library of Congress Cataloging-in-Publication Data
Roberts, Lee, 1941–
    Praying God's will for my wife / Lee Roberts.
        p.   cm.
    ISBN 0-8407-9177-1 (pbk.)
    1. Husbands—Prayer-books and devotions—English.   2. Wives—Religious life.   3. Christian life—1960–   I. Title.
BV283.H8R63   1993
242'.842—dc20

92-35596
CIP

1 2 3 4 5 6 — 97 96 95 94 93 92

Contents

For Men Only

The single most important thing that you can do for your wife is to pray for her. Praying for your wife is more than a privilege. It is a responsibility and one that you, as her husband, must not take lightly.

Properly praying for the wife that God has given you is a two-step process. The first step is committing to pray for her on a daily basis. The second step is knowing what to pray. Observe your wife. Listen to her. See and hear what her needs are. Learn her strengths and her weaknesses. And then pray for her in each of these areas. More than that, pray God's perfect will for your wife. You do that by praying what God has already declared in His Word to be His perfect will.

On the pages that follow you will find, in the form of special prayers for your wife, God's will for her in every area of her life. Each of these prayers comes directly from Scripture. Because of that, they are the most powerful prayers that you can pray for the one that God has entrusted to you as your helpmate.

Begin today to pray God's Word over your wife on a daily basis, and you will soon see dynamic growth take place in her life, in your marriage, and in her as the wife that God desires her to be.

1

ANGER

⌣

Heavenly Father, I thank You for all that You do for my wife and me. During this time of being alone with You I ask You, in the name of Jesus, to hear Your word as my prayers concerning any anger that may abide in my wife. Your word is clear that anger does not produce the righteousness that You want in each of us. I petition You now, with Your very words, to remove any anger from my wife that may be a stumbling block in her walk with You. Thank You, God, for answering my prayers.

**God, in accordance
with Your Word...**

I pray that my wife will be swift to hear, slow to speak, slow to wrath; for her wrath does not produce the righteousness of God.

JAMES 1:19–20

I pray that the discretion of my wife makes her slow to anger, and it is to her glory to overlook a transgression.

PROVERBS 19:11

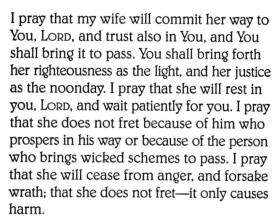

I pray that my wife will commit her way to You, LORD, and trust also in You, and You shall bring it to pass. You shall bring forth her righteousness as the light, and her justice as the noonday. I pray that she will rest in you, LORD, and wait patiently for you. I pray that she does not fret because of him who prospers in his way or because of the person who brings wicked schemes to pass. I pray that she will cease from anger, and forsake wrath; that she does not fret—it only causes harm.

PSALM 37:5–8

I pray that my wife will not hasten in her spirit to be angry, for anger rests in the bosom of fools.

ECCLESIASTES 7:9

I pray that my wife will let all bitterness, wrath, anger, clamor, and evil speaking be put away from her, with all malice. I pray also that she will be kind to others, tenderhearted, forgiving others, just as God in Christ also forgave her.

EPHESIANS 4:31–32

❤

I pray that my wife understands that a fool vents all his feelings, but a wise person holds theirs back.

PROVERBS 29:11

❤

I pray that my wife knows that being slow to anger is better than the mighty, and ruling her spirit is better than taking a city.

PROVERBS 16:32

❤

I pray that my wife realizes that a person who is quick-tempered acts foolishly.

PROVERBS 14:17

I pray that if my wife is angry, she will not sin. That she does not let the sun go down on her wrath.

EPHESIANS 4:26

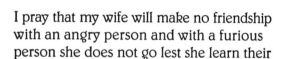

I pray that my wife will make no friendship with an angry person and with a furious person she does not go lest she learn their ways and sets a snare for her soul.

PROVERBS 22:24–25

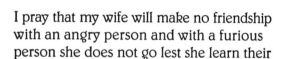

I pray that my wife always remembers that a soft answer turns away wrath, but a harsh word stirs up anger.

PROVERBS 15:1

2

ATTITUDE

Lord Jesus, I ask You now, using the very words that have been given to me in the Holy Scriptures, to make certain that my wife always has an attitude of joy in You and an expectancy that she can do all things through You. Thank You, Lord, for her happiness and her joy. In Your name I pray. Amen.

God, in accordance with Your Word...

I pray that my wife knows that she can do all things through Christ who strengthens her.

PHILIPPIANS 4:13

———— ♥ ————

I pray that my wife will not sorrow, for the joy of the LORD is her strength.

NEHEMIAH 8:10

I pray that my wife will remember whatever things are true, whatever things are noble, whatever things are just, whatever things are pure, whatever things are lovely, whatever things are of good report, if there is any virtue and if there is anything praiseworthy— that she will meditate on these things.

PHILIPPIANS 4:8

♥

I pray that my wife will remember that this is the day which the LORD has made and that she will rejoice and be glad in it.

PSALM 118:24

♥

I pray that my wife will always love You, the LORD her God, with all her heart, with all her soul, with all her mind, and with all her strength and that she will love her neighbor as herself.

MARK 12:30–31

I pray that my wife understands what Jesus meant when He said, "My grace is sufficient for you, for My strength is made perfect in weakness."

2 CORINTHIANS 12:9

♥

I pray that my wife realizes that in all these things she is more than a conqueror through You who loved her.

ROMANS 8:37

♥

I pray that whatever my wife does she does it heartily, as to You, Lord, and not to men.

COLOSSIANS 3:23

3

CONDEMNED

Lord God, I come before You at this moment to ask You to keep in my wife's mind at all times that there is no condemnation for those who are in Christ Jesus. Help her to know that if she trusts in Jesus she need not allow doubt to be in her mind. Thank You, Lord, for removing all such thoughts and feelings from my wife. Thank You in Jesus' name. Amen.

God, in accordance with Your Word...

I pray that my wife will draw near with a true heart in full assurance of faith, having her heart sprinkled from an evil conscience and her body washed with pure water.

HEBREWS 10:22

♥

I pray that my wife always remembers that You, the LORD her God, are gracious and

merciful, and will not turn Your face from
her if she returns to You.

2 CHRONICLES 30:9

———————— ♥ ————————

I pray that my wife knows that it was You,
God, who said that, "I, even I, am He who
blots out your transgressions for My own
sake."

ISAIAH 43:25

———————— ♥ ————————

I pray, God, that You did not send Your Son
into the world to condemn my wife, but that
my wife through Him might be saved. She
who believes in Him is not condemned.

JOHN 3:17–18

———————— ♥ ————————

I pray that my wife, who hears Your word
and believes in Him who sent You, has
everlasting life, and shall not come into

judgment, but has passed from death into life.

JOHN 5:24

♥

I pray that You, God, will be merciful to my wife's unrighteousness, and to her sins and to her lawless deeds and that You remember them no more.

HEBREWS 8:12

♥

I pray that my wife will forsake any wicked ways and any unrighteous thoughts. Let her return to You, LORD, and You will have mercy on her and abundantly pardon her.

ISAIAH 55:7

♥

I pray that my wife will acknowledge her sin to You, God, and her iniquity she has not hidden. That she will confess her transgressions to You so You can forgive the iniquity of her sins.

PSALM 32:5

♥

I pray that if my wife will confess her sins, You, God, are faithful and just to forgive her sins and to cleanse her from all unrighteousness.

1 JOHN 1:9

♥

I pray that as far as the east is from the west, so far have You removed my wife's transgressions from her.

PSALM 103:12

♥

I pray that there is therefore now no condemnation to my wife who is in Christ Jesus, who does not walk according to the flesh, but according to the Spirit. For the law

of the Spirit of life in Christ Jesus has made
her free from the law of sin and death.

ROMANS 8:1–2

———— ♥ ————

I pray that if my wife is in You, Christ, she
is a new creation; old things have passed
away; behold, all things have become new.

2 CORINTHIANS 5:17

———— ♥ ————

I pray that my wife is blessed, whose
transgression is forgiven, whose sin is
covered.

PSALM 32:1

———— ♥ ————

I pray that my wife has overcome Satan by
the blood of the Lamb and by the word of
her testimony.

REVELATION 12:11

I pray that my wife remembers that Jesus Himself said, "Neither do I condemn you; go and sin no more."

JOHN 8:11

—— ♥ ——

I pray, God, that You will forgive my wife's iniquity and her sin and will remember them no more.

JEREMIAH 31:34

4

CONFIDENCE

Lord Jesus, based upon God's word I call upon You to fill my wife with confidence. Give her the spiritual confidence to know that whatever she asks in Your name she will receive. Fill her with the confidence that only You can give. Thank You for honoring Your word and my prayers. Amen.

God, in accordance with Your Word...

I pray that when my wife passes through the waters, You will be with her; and through the rivers, they shall not overflow her. When she walks through the fire, she shall not be burned, nor shall the flame scorch her. For You are the LORD her God.

ISAIAH 43:2–3

———— ♥ ————

I pray, God, that my wife always remembers that it is You who justifies.

ROMANS 8:33

I pray that this is the confidence that my wife has in You, Jesus, that if she asks anything according to Your will, You hear her. And if she knows that You hear her, whatever she asks, she knows that she has the petitions that she asked of You.

1 JOHN 5:14–15

♥

I pray that when my wife faces an obstacle she always remembers that God has said that it is "Not by might nor by power, but by My Spirit."

ZECHARIAH 4:6

♥

I pray that whatever my wife asks in Jesus name, You will do it.

JOHN 14:14

♥

I pray that You, the LORD God, are my wife's strength.

HABAKKUK 3:19

I pray that my wife will not cast away her confidence, which has great reward. For she has need of endurance, so that after she has done the will of You, God, she may receive the promise.

HEBREWS 10:35–36

———— ♥ ————

I pray that my wife will be confident of this very thing, that You who have begun a good work in her will complete it until the day of Jesus Christ.

PHILIPPIANS 1:6

———— ♥ ————

I pray that my wife can do all things through Christ who strengthens her.

PHILIPPIANS 4:13

———— ♥ ————

I pray that my wife may boldly say: "The LORD is my helper; I will not fear. What can man do to me?"

HEBREWS 13:6

I pray that if my wife's heart does not condemn her, she will have confidence toward You, God.

1 JOHN 3:21

❤

I pray that if my wife will wait on You, LORD, she shall renew her strength. She shall mount up with wings like eagles, she shall run and not be weary, she shall walk and not faint.

ISAIAH 40:31

5

CONFUSED

Heavenly Father, in the beautiful and precious name of Jesus, my Lord and Savior, I ask You to remove all confusion from my wife. Help her to know that You are the author of peace and that she is to lean on You and Your word. Thank You for honoring this my prayer for my wonderful and precious wife. Amen.

God, in accordance with Your Word...

I pray that my wife will trust in You, LORD, with all her heart, and lean not on her own understanding. I pray that in all her ways she will acknowledge You, and You will direct her paths.

PROVERBS 3:5–6

———— ♥ ————

I pray that You, God, will instruct my wife and teach her in the way she should go.

PSALM 32:8

I pray that my wife has great peace because she loves Your law, and nothing can cause her to stumble.

PSALM 119:165

———— ♥ ————

I pray that my wife will always cast her burdens on You, LORD, and You shall sustain her.

PSALM 55:22

———— ♥ ————

I pray that when my wife passes through the waters, You will be with her. And when she passes through the rivers, they shall not overflow her. When she walks through the fire, she shall not be burned, nor shall the flame scorch her. For You are the LORD her God.

ISAIAH 43:2–3

———— ♥ ————

I pray that my wife will be anxious for nothing, but in everything by prayer and supplication, with thanksgiving, let her requests be made known to You, God, and the peace of God, which surpasses all understanding, will guard her heart and mind through Christ Jesus.

PHILIPPIANS 4:6–7

———— ♥ ————

I pray that my wife will always remember that God gives power to the weak, and to those who have no might He increases strength.

ISAIAH 40:29

———— ♥ ————

I pray that when my wife feels confused she will remember and understand that You, God, are not the author of confusion but of peace.

1 CORINTHIANS 14:33

———— ♥ ————

I pray, God, that You have not given my wife a spirit of fear, but of power and of love and of a sound mind.

1 TIMOTHY 1:7

I pray that my wife knows that where envy and self-seeking exist, confusion and every evil thing will be there. But the wisdom that is from above is first pure, then peaceable, gentle, willing to yield, full of mercy and good fruits, without partiality and without hypocrisy.

JAMES 3:16–17

I pray that You, Lord GOD, will help my wife; therefore she will not be disgraced.

ISAIAH 50:7

I pray that my wife will not think it strange concerning the fiery trial which is to try her, as though some strange thing happened to her; but that she will rejoice to the extent that she partakes of Christ's sufferings, that when her glory is revealed, she also may be glad with exceeding joy.

1 PETER 4:12–13

I pray that if my wife lacks wisdom, let her ask of You, God, who gives to all liberally and without reproach, and it will be given to her.

JAMES 1:5

6

COURAGE

Perfect God, grant my wife the courage that only You can give. Help her to remember that You promised in Your word that she can do all things through Jesus and that she should never be afraid or discouraged or dismayed because You, her God, will be with her always. Thank You, God, in Jesus' name, for filling my wife with courage. Amen.

God, in accordance with Your Word...

I pray that my wife will always fear not, for You, God, are with her. I pray that she will not be dismayed, for You are her God. I pray that You will strengthen her and help her and that You will uphold her with Your righteous right hand.

ISAIAH 41:10

I pray that my wife will be persuaded that neither death nor life, nor angels nor principalities nor powers, nor things present nor things to come, nor height nor depth, nor any other created thing, shall be able to separate her from the love of God which is in Christ Jesus her Lord.

ROMANS 8:38–39

♥

I pray that my wife shall not die, but live, and declare the works of the LORD.

PSALM 118:17

♥

I pray that You, the eternal God, are my wife's refuge and that You will thrust out the enemy from before her.

DEUTERONOMY 33:27

♥

I pray that my wife can do all things through Christ who strengthens her.

PHILIPPIANS 4:13

I pray that my wife will wait on You, LORD;
that she will be of good courage, and You
shall strengthen her heart.

PSALM 27:14

I pray that my wife does not think it strange
concerning the fiery trial which is to try her,
as though some strange thing happened to
her; but that she will rejoice to the extent
that she partakes of Christ's sufferings, that
when her glory is revealed, she may also
be glad with exceeding joy.

1 PETER 4:12–13

I pray that when my wife passes through
the waters, You will be with her; and through
the rivers, they shall not overflow her. When
she walks through the fire, she shall not be
burned, nor shall the flame scorch her. For
You are the LORD her God.

ISAIAH 43:2–3

I pray that while my wife's weeping may endure for a night, joy comes to her in the morning.

PSALM 30:5

♥

I pray that my wife will be of good courage, and that You shall strengthen her heart, for her hope is in You, Lord.

PSALM 31:24

♥

I pray that my wife will wait on You, Lord, and that she shall renew her strength. I pray that she shall mount up with wings like eagles; that she shall run and not be weary; that she shall walk and not faint.

ISAIAH 40:31

♥

I pray that my wife will be anxious for nothing, but in everything by prayer and supplication, with thanksgiving, will let her requests be made known to You, God.

PHILIPPIANS 4:6

♥

I pray that whatever things are true, whatever things are noble, whatever things are just, whatever things are pure, whatever things are lovely, whatever things are of good report, if there is any virtue and if there is anything praiseworthy—that my wife will meditate on these things.

PHILIPPIANS 4:8

♥

I pray that my wife shall obtain joy and gladness and that sorrow and sighing shall flee away.

ISAIAH 51:11

7

DELIVERANCE

Lord Jesus, today, at this very moment, I ask You to deliver my wife from anything that is adversely affecting her. Help her to know the truth that comes only from You and Your word and to be set free from all that is upon her. Thank You, Jesus, for freeing my wife and for filling her with joy and hope. Amen.

God, in accordance with Your Word...

I pray that my wife shall know the truth, and the truth shall make her free.

JOHN 8:32

———— ♥ ————

I pray that if You, Jesus, make my wife free, she shall be free indeed.

JOHN 8:36

I pray that there is therefore now no condemnation to my wife who is in Christ Jesus, who does not walk according to the flesh, but according to the Spirit. For the law of the Spirit of life in Christ Jesus has made her free from the law of sin and death.

ROMANS 8:1–2

❤

I pray that my wife does not believe every spirit, but that she tests the spirits, whether they are of You, God; because many false prophets have gone out into the world. I pray that by this she will know the Spirit of God: that every spirit that confesses that Jesus Christ has come in the flesh is of God, and every spirit that does not confess that Jesus Christ has come in the flesh is not of God.

1 JOHN 4:1–3

❤

I pray that He who is in my wife is greater than he who is in the world.

1 JOHN 4:4

I pray that my wife has overcome Satan by the blood of the Lamb and by the word of her testimony.

REVELATION 12:11

8

DEPRESSED

Lord God, I pray to You now as always in Jesus' name. I ask You to remove any depression that may come upon my wife at any time. Help her to know that if she cries out to You that You will hear. I ask You to honor Your word and deliver her from any depression that she may ever experience. In Jesus' name, Amen.

God, in accordance
with Your Word...

I pray that my righteous wife will cry out, and You will hear and deliver her out of all of her troubles.

PSALM 34:17

♥

I pray, God, that You are the God of my wife's strength.

PSALM 43:2

I pray that while my wife's weeping may endure for a night, her joy comes in the morning.

PSALM 30:5

———— ♥ ————

I pray that my wife will wait on You, LORD. That she shall renew her strength. That she shall mount up with wings like eagles; that she shall run and not be weary and that she shall walk and not faint.

ISAIAH 40:31

———— ♥ ————

I pray, God, that you will comfort my wife in all her tribulation, that she may be able to comfort those who are in any trouble, with the comfort with which she herself is comforted by You.

2 CORINTHIANS 1:4

———— ♥ ————

I pray that neither death nor life, nor angels nor principalities nor powers, nor things present nor things to come, nor height nor depth, nor any other created thing, shall be able to separate my wife from Your love, God, which is in Christ Jesus her Lord.

ROMANS 8:38–39

♥

I pray that my wife does not think it strange concerning the fiery trial which is to try her, as though some strange thing happened to her; but that she will rejoice to the extent that she partakes of Christ's sufferings, so that when her glory is revealed, she may also be glad with exceeding joy.

1 PETER 4:12–13

♥

I pray that whatever things are true, whatever things are noble, whatever things are just, whatever things are pure, whatever things are lovely, whatever things are of good report, if there is any virtue and if there is anything praiseworthy—that my wife will meditate on these things.

PHILIPPIANS 4:8

I pray, God, that You will heal my wife's broken heart and bind up her wounds.

PSALM 147:3

———— ♥ ————

I pray that my wife will fear not, for You are with her. That she will not be dismayed, for You are her God. I pray that You will strengthen her; that You will help her and that You will uphold her with Your righteous right hand.

ISAIAH 41:10

———— ♥ ————

I pray that my wife will humble herself under the mighty hand of God, that You may exalt her in due time. I pray that she will cast all her cares upon You, for You care for her.

1 PETER 5:6–7

———— ♥ ————

I pray that my wife will always pray and not lose heart.

LUKE 18:1

I pray that my wife will not sorrow, for the joy of the LORD is her strength.

NEHEMIAH 8:10

9

DESERTED BY LOVED ONES

Heavenly Father, I plead with You at this moment to honor Your word and set my wife on high. Your word has promised that You will never leave her or forsake her, no matter what her loved ones might do. She needs You now. Draw her close to You and carry her burdens for her. In the name of Your Son, Jesus, I pray. Amen.

God, in accordance with Your Word...

I pray that because You have set Your love upon my wife, You will deliver her. You will set her on high, because she has known Your name. I pray that she shall call upon You and You will answer her. That you will be with her in trouble. That You will deliver her and honor her. That with long life You will satisfy her and show her Your salvation.

PSALM 91:14–16

I pray, God, that You will not forsake my wife
nor destroy her.

DEUTERONOMY 4:31

---------- ♥ ----------

I pray that You, God, will hear my wife and
that You will not forsake her.

ISAIAH 41:17

---------- ♥ ----------

I pray that my wife will cast all her cares
upon You, God, for You care for her.

1 PETER 5:7

---------- ♥ ----------

I pray that while my wife is hard pressed
on every side, yet she is not crushed; she
is perplexed, but not in despair; persecuted,
but not forsaken; struck down, but not
destroyed—always carrying about in her
body the dying of the Lord Jesus, that the
life of Jesus also may be manifested in her
body.

2 CORINTHIANS 4:8–10

I pray that my wife will no longer be forsaken and You will delight in her.

ISAIAH 62:4

———— ♥ ————

I pray that because my wife knows Your name, God, she will put her trust in You; for You, LORD, have not forsaken those who seek You.

PSALM 9:10

———— ♥ ————

I pray that if my wife's father and my mother forsake her that You will take care of her.

PSALM 27:10

———— ♥ ————

I pray that my wife will be taught to observe all things that Jesus has commanded and that she knows that You are with her always, even to the end of the age.

MATTHEW 28:20

I pray that my wife always remembers that
You will not forget her.

ISAIAH 49:15

♥

I pray that my wife's hope is in You, God,
and that she shall yet praise You, the help
of her countenance and her God.

PSALM 43:5

♥

I pray that my wife will be strong and of
good courage. That she will not fear nor be
afraid; for You, the LORD her God, are the
One who goes with her. I know that You
will not leave her or forsake her.

DEUTERONOMY 31:6

♥

I pray that You will not forsake my wife, for
Your great name's sake, because it has
pleased You to make her one of Your people.

1 SAMUEL 12:22

10

DISCOURAGED

Perfect God, in Jesus' name I ask You to remove from my wife any discouragement that she may be feeling at this time in her life. Teach her to wait on You and to be of good courage. Teach her that You will strengthen her. Thank You for hearing and honoring Your words. Amen.

God, in accordance
with Your Word...

I pray that my wife will wait on You, LORD; that she will be of good courage and that You will strengthen her heart.

PSALM 27:14

❤

I pray that my wife will be of good courage and that You, God, shall strengthen her heart.

PSALM 31:24

I pray that my wife shall obtain joy and gladness and that sorrow and sighing shall flee away.

ISAIAH 51:11

♥

I pray that my wife will not cast away her confidence, which has great reward. For she has need of endurance, so that after she has done Your will, God, she may receive her promise.

HEBREWS 10:35–36

♥

I pray that my wife is confident of this very thing, that You, God, who have begun a good work in her will complete it until the day of Jesus Christ.

PHILIPPIANS 1:6

♥

I pray that my wife will greatly rejoice, though now for a little while, if need be, she may be grieved by various trials. I pray that

the genuineness of her faith, being much
more precious than gold that perishes,
though it is tested by fire, may be found to
praise, honor, and glory at the revelation
of Jesus Christ, whom having not seen, she
loves. Though now she does not see Him,
yet believing, she rejoices with joy
inexpressible and full of glory, receiving the
end of her faith—the salvation of her soul.

1 PETER 1:6–9

———— ♥ ————

I pray that my wife does not grow weary
while doing good, for in due season she shall
reap if she does not lose heart.

GALATIANS 6:9

———— ♥ ————

I pray that in everything my wife will be
anxious for nothing, but in everything by
prayer and supplication, with thanksgiving,
lets her request be made known to You, God;
and Your peace, which surpasses all
understanding, will guard her heart and
mind through Christ Jesus. And, God,

whatever things are true, whatever things are noble, whatever things are just, whatever things are pure, whatever things are lovely, whatever things are of good report, if there is any virtue and if there is anything praiseworthy—help her to meditate on these things.

PHILIPPIANS 4:6–8

♥

I pray, God, though my wife walks in the midst of trouble, You will revive her. You will stretch out Your hand against the wrath of her enemies. I pray that with Your right hand You will save her.

PSALM 138:7

♥

I pray that my wife will always understand and believe Your promise, Jesus, that Your peace You left with her and that Your peace You gave to her and that not as the world gives did You give it to her. Let not her heart be troubled, neither let it be afraid.

JOHN 14:27

I pray that my wife will not let her heart be troubled. That she will believe in You, God, and also in Jesus.

JOHN 14:1

———— ♥ ————

I pray that while my wife is hard pressed on every side, she is not crushed, she is perplexed, but not in despair; persecuted, but not forsaken; struck down, but not destroyed—always carrying about in her body the dying of the Lord Jesus, that the life of Jesus also may be manifested in her body.

2 CORINTHIANS 4:8–10

11

DISSATISFIED

Lord Jesus, through the power of Your perfect and error-free word I call upon You to replace any dissatisfaction in my wife's life with joy, hope, and happiness. Your word says her soul will be satisfied and she shall have every good thing. Through my faith and the authority of Your word, I now pray Your word for my wife and ask that You hear and honor these words from Your word in the Bible. Thank You for hearing my prayers. Amen.

God, in accordance with Your Word...

I pray that my wife can do all things through Christ who strengthens her.

PHILIPPIANS 4:13

♥

I pray that my wife will be satisfied with good by the fruit of her mouth.

PROVERBS 12:14

I pray that my wife's soul shall be satisfied as with marrow and fatness, and her mouth shall praise You with joyful lips.

PSALM 63:5

———— ♥ ————

I pray that because my wife seeks You, LORD, she shall not lack any good thing.

PSALM 34:10

———— ♥ ————

I pray that my wife will delight herself in You, LORD, and You shall give her the desires of her heart.

PSALM 37:4

———— ♥ ————

I pray that my wife will bless You, LORD, with all that is within her and that she will forget not all Your benefits. I pray that she will not forget who forgives all her iniquities and who heals all her diseases. I pray that she will not forget who redeems her life from destruction and who crowns her with lovingkindness and tender mercies and who satisfies her mouth with good things, so that her youth is renewed like the eagle's.

PSALM 103:1–5

———— ♥ ————

I pray, God, that You will satisfy my wife's longing soul and fill her hungry soul with goodness.

PSALM 107:9

———— ♥ ————

I pray that my wife will trust and not be afraid; for You, God, are her strength and her song. You have become her salvation.

ISAIAH 12:2

———— ♥ ————

I pray that You, God, who supply seed to the sower and bread for food, will supply and multiply the seed my wife has sown and will increase the fruits of her righteousness.

2 CORINTHIANS 9:10

12

DISTRESS / SADNESS

God in heaven, You have promised the comfort of the Holy Spirit to us in times such as this. I ask You for a special comforting for my wife. Your word says that even though sadness may come upon her, her joy will return in the morning. I pray this, Your word, for my wife. Remove her distress. Take her sadness. And honor these Your words that I am about to pray. Thank You in Jesus' name. Amen.

God, in accordance with Your Word...

I pray that my wife has done justice and righteousness and that You will not leave her to her oppressors.

PSALM 119:121

♥

I pray that while my wife may be despised, she does not forget Your precepts.

PSALM 119:141

I pray that while trouble and anguish have overtaken my wife, Your commandments are her delights. The righteousness of Your testimonies is everlasting. I pray that You will give her understanding, and she shall live.

PSALM 119:143–144

I pray that in righteousness my wife shall be established. That she shall be far from oppression, for she shall not fear; and from terror, for it shall not come near her.

ISAIAH 54:14

I pray that You, God, will strengthen my wife according to Your word.

PSALM 119:28

I pray that it is good for my wife that she has been afflicted so that she can learn Your statutes.

PSALM 119:71

I pray that You, God, will consider my wife's affliction and deliver her, for she does not forget Your law. I pray that You will plead her cause and redeem her. Revive her according to Your word.

PSALM 119:153–154

♥

I pray that my wife has great peace because she loves Your law, God, and nothing causes her to stumble.

PSALM 119:165

♥

I pray that if my wife has gone astray like a lost sheep, that You, God, will seek her, Your servant, and not let her forget Your commandments.

PSALM 119:176

♥

I pray that my wife will always pray "Blessed be the Lord," who daily loads her with benefits.

PSALM 68:19

I pray, God, that You will bring my wife up out of a horrible pit and out of the miry clay. Set her feet upon a rock and establish her steps.

PSALM 40:2

———— ♥ ————

I pray that You, God, are my wife's refuge and strength, a very present help in trouble, and that she will not fear.

PSALM 46:1–2

———— ♥ ————

I pray that since Your name, LORD, is a strong tower, that my righteous wife runs to it and is safe.

PROVERBS 18:10

———— ♥ ————

I pray that my wife will not let her heart be troubled and that she will always believe in God and in Jesus.

JOHN 14:1

I pray that my wife will not sorrow, for the joy of the Lord is her strength.

NEHEMIAH 8:10

I pray that my wife will always live with the realization that her Lord is faithful and will establish her and guard her from the evil one.

2 THESSALONIANS 3:3

13

DON'T UNDERSTAND GOD

Lord God, the words that I am about to pray are
Your words. Hear them, please, and honor them.
Help my wife to understand that she may not always
understand Your thoughts and Your way. Remind
her of Your promise that if she calls upon You, You
will tell her great and unsearchable things. I now
pray Your word to You in Jesus' name. Amen.

God, in accordance
with Your Word...

I pray that You, God, will help my wife to
understand that Your thoughts are not her
thoughts nor are her ways Your ways. That
she will understand that as the heavens
are higher than the earth, so are Your
ways higher than her ways and Your
thoughts higher than her thoughts.

ISAIAH 55:8–9

I pray that my wife will call to You, God,
and that You will answer her and show her
great and mighty things, which she does not
know.

JEREMIAH 33:3

———— ♥ ————

I pray that if You, God, are for my wife, who
can be against her?

ROMANS 8:31

———— ♥ ————

I pray that in all things my wife is more than
a conqueror through Him who loved her.

ROMANS 8:37

———— ♥ ————

I pray that my wife will pursue the
knowledge of the LORD.

HOSEA 6:3

I pray that as for You, God, Your way is perfect. The word of the LORD is proven; You are a shield to my wife who trusts in You.

PSALM 18:30

♥

I pray, God, that You will perfect that which concerns my wife and that your mercy, O LORD, endures forever.

PSALM 138:8

♥

I pray that You, God, will make an everlasting covenant with my wife, that You will not turn away from doing her good; but that You will put Your fear in her heart so that she will not depart from You.

JEREMIAH 32:40

♥

I pray that my wife will hold fast the confession of her hope without wavering, for You, God, who promised are faithful.

HEBREWS 10:23

I pray that all things work together for good
to my wife who loves You, God, to her who
was called according to Your purpose.

ROMANS 8:28

———— ♥ ————

I pray that no temptation has overtaken my
wife except such as is common to man; but
You, God, are faithful, who will not allow
her to be tempted beyond what she is able,
but with the temptation You will also make
the way of escape, that she may be able to
bear it.

1 CORINTHIANS 10:13

———— ♥ ————

I pray that while many are the afflictions of
the righteous wife, You, LORD deliver her
out of them all.

PSALM 34:19

———— ♥ ————

I pray that my wife will cast her burden on
You, LORD, and You shall sustain her.

PSALM 55:22

I pray that my wife will fear not, for You,
God, are with her. That she will not be
dismayed, for You are her God. That You
will strengthen her and help her. That You
will uphold her with Your righteous right
hand.

ISAIAH 41:10

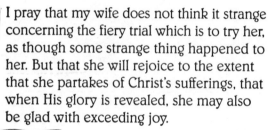

I pray that my wife does not think it strange
concerning the fiery trial which is to try her,
as though some strange thing happened to
her. But that she will rejoice to the extent
that she partakes of Christ's sufferings, that
when His glory is revealed, she may also
be glad with exceeding joy.

1 PETER 4:12–13

14

DOUBTING GOD

Heavenly Father, today I pray the power of Your perfect word to remove any doubts about You that my wife might have. Your way is perfect and Your word is proven. Use Your Holy Spirit to impart Your perfection to my wife and to remove any doubts that she may have now or at any time in her life. Help her more than ever to believe and not doubt. In Jesus' name I pray. Amen.

God, in accordance with Your Word...

I pray that because Your way is perfect and Your word is proven; that You, God, are a shield to my wife who trusts in You.

PSALM 18:30

❤

I pray, God, that my wife will always remember that Your hand is not shortened so that it cannot save; nor Your ear heavy, that it cannot hear.

ISAIAH 59:1

———— ♥ ————

I pray that You, Lord, are not slack concerning Your promise, as some count slackness, but are longsuffering toward my wife, not willing that she should perish but that she should come to repentance.

2 PETER 3:9

———— ♥ ————

I pray, God, that my wife is aware that You have said Your counsel shall stand and You will do all Your pleasure. Indeed, You have spoken it and You will also bring it to pass. You have purposed it and You will also do it.

ISAIAH 46:10–11

———— ♥ ————

I pray that my wife does not seek what she should eat or what she should drink, nor

have an anxious mind. For all these things
the nations of the world seek after, and You,
her Father, know that she needs these things.
I pray that she will seek the kingdom of God,
and all these things shall be added to her.

LUKE 12:29–31

♥

I pray that my wife knows that He who calls
her is faithful, who also will do it.

1 THESSALONIANS 5:24

♥

I pray that whatever things my wife asks for
when she prays, that she will believe that
she will receive them, and she will have
them.

MARK 11:24

♥

I pray that my wife will always remember
that You, God, have declared that, "So shall
My word be that goes forth from My mouth.
It shall not return to Me void. But it shall

accomplish what I please, and it shall
prosper in the thing for which I sent it."

ISAIAH 55:11

———— ♥ ————

I pray that my wife knows that faith comes
by hearing and hearing by the word of God.

ROMANS 10:17

———— ♥ ————

I pray that my wife does not think it strange
concerning the fiery trial which is to try her,
as though some strange thing happened to
her. But that she rejoices to the extent that
she partakes of Christ's sufferings, that when
His glory is revealed, she may also be glad
with exceeding joy.

1 PETER 4:12–13

15

EMOTIONALLY UPSET

Jesus, I am here to pray Your word and to ask You to give great peace to my wife. She loves You. Give her a sound mind and a peace that passes all understanding. Let her be anxious for nothing. Thank you, Jesus, for honoring Your word in this important time in my wife's life. Amen.

God, in accordance with Your Word...

I pray that my wife will have great peace because she loves Your law and nothing causes her to stumble.

PSALM 119:165

❤

I pray that because my wife believes in You, God, she will by no means be put to shame.

1 PETER 2:6

I pray that You, God, will help my wife;
therefore she will not be disgraced. She can
set her face like a flint and know that she
will not be ashamed.

ISAIAH 50:7

♥

I pray that You, God, have not given my wife
a spirit of fear, but of power and of love and
of a sound mind.

2 TIMOTHY 1:7

♥

I pray that my wife will fear not, for You,
God, are with her. That she be not dismayed,
for You are her God. I pray that You will
strengthen her and help her and that You
will uphold her with Your righteous right
hand.

ISAIAH 41:10

♥

I pray that my wife will be anxious for
nothing, but in everything by prayer and

supplication, with thanksgiving, will let her
requests be made known to You, God, and
Your peace, God, which surpasses all
understanding, will guard her heart and
mind through Christ Jesus.

PHILIPPIANS 4:6–7

♥

I pray that my wife will cast her burden on
You, LORD, and that You will sustain her.

PSALM 55:22

♥

I pray that my wife will realize that You, God,
are not the author of confusion but of peace.

1 CORINTHIANS 14:33

♥

I pray that my wife knows that where envy
and self-seeking exist, confusion and every
evil thing will be there. I pray that she will
also know that the wisdom that is from

above is first pure, then peaceable, gentle, willing to yield, full of mercy and good fruits, without partiality and without hypocrisy and that the fruit of righteousness is sown in peace by those who make peace.

JAMES 3:16–18

♥

I pray that while my wife's weeping may endure for a night, her joy comes in the morning.

PSALM 30:5

♥

I pray that when my wife passes through the waters, You, God, will be with her. And when she passes through the rivers, they shall not overflow her. I pray that when she walks through the fire, she shall not be burned, nor shall the flame scorch her. You are the LORD her God.

ISAIAH 43:2–3

I pray that You, God, will comfort my wife
in all her tribulation, that she may be able
to comfort those who are in any trouble,
with the comfort with which she herself is
comforted by You.

2 CORINTHIANS 1:4

——————— ♥ ———————

I pray that You, God, will heal my wife's
broken heart and bind up her wounds.

PSALM 147:3

——————— ♥ ———————

I pray that whatever things are true,
whatever things are noble, whatever things
are just, whatever things are pure, whatever
things are lovely, whatever things are of good
report, if there is any virtue and if there is
anything praiseworthy—that my wife will
meditate on these things.

PHILIPPIANS 4:8

——————— ♥ ———————

I pray that neither death nor life, nor angels
nor principalities nor powers, nor things

present nor things to come, nor height nor
depth, nor any other created thing, shall be
able to separate my wife from the love of
God which is in Christ Jesus her Lord.

ROMANS 8:38–39

16

FAITH

Father God, in the name of Your Son, Jesus, I pray to You Your perfect word for my wife. Increase her faith. Help her to remember that You said she is to walk by faith and not by sight. Hear and answer Your word now concerning my wife's faith. Thank You. In Jesus' name. Amen.

God, in accordance with Your Word...

I pray that You, Lord, will increase my wife's faith.

LUKE 17:5

I pray that my wife's faith comes by hearing, and hearing by the word of God.

ROMANS 10:17

I pray that my wife will walk by faith and
not by sight.

2 CORINTHIANS 5:7

───── ♥ ─────

I pray that my wife will have a pure heart,
a good conscience, and sincere faith.

1 TIMOTHY 1:5

───── ♥ ─────

I pray that my wife will always remember
that faith is the substance of things hoped
for and the evidence of things not seen.

HEBREWS 11:1

───── ♥ ─────

I pray that my wife remembers that faith
by itself, if it does not have works, is dead.

JAMES 2:17

───── ♥ ─────

I pray that my wife will constantly take the
shield of faith with which she will be able

to quench all the fiery darts of the wicked
one.

EPHESIANS 6:16

———— ♥ ————

I pray that my wife will put on the
breastplate of faith and love, and as her
helmet the hope of salvation.

1 THESSALONIANS 5:8

———— ♥ ————

I pray that my wife will always have faith
and a good conscience.

1 TIMOTHY 1:19

———— ♥ ————

I pray my wife will draw near with a true
heart in the full assurance of her faith and
that she will have her heart sprinkled from
an evil conscience and her body washed
with pure water.

HEBREWS 10:22

I pray that my wife will fight the good fight
of faith, that she will lay hold on eternal life,
to which she was also called.

1 TIMOTHY 6:12

♥

I pray that my wife understands that without
faith it is impossible to please You, God, and
that for her to come to You she must believe
that You are and that You are a rewarder
of those who diligently seek You.

HEBREWS 11:6

♥

I pray that my wife will be just and will live
by faith.

HABAKKUK 2:4

♥

I pray that my wife will remember that
Abraham believed God, and it was
accounted to him for righteousness.

ROMANS 4:3

I pray that my wife, having been justified
by faith, will have peace with You, God,
through her Lord Jesus Christ.

ROMANS 5:1

———— ♥ ————

I pray that my wife will count all things as
a loss for the excellence of the knowledge
of Christ Jesus her Lord, for whom she has
suffered the loss of all things, and count them
as rubbish, that she may gain Christ and be
found in Him, not having her own
righteousness, which is from the law, but that
which is through faith in Christ, the
righteousness which is from God by faith;
that she may know Him and the power of
His resurrection, and the fellowship of His
sufferings, being conformed to His death.

PHILIPPIANS 3:8–10

———— ♥ ————

I pray that my wife will be just and will live
by faith.

HEBREWS 10:38

I pray that my wife shall believe in You, the LORD her God, and she shall be established. I pray also that she will believe Your prophets and she shall prosper.

2 CHRONICLES 20:20

———— ♥ ————

I pray that according to my wife's faith, it will be to her.

MATTHEW 9:29

———— ♥ ————

I pray that my wife will have faith as a mustard seed and she will say to her mountain, "Move from here to there," and it will move, and nothing will be impossible to her.

MATTHEW 17:20

———— ♥ ————

I pray that my wife will have faith in You, God.

MARK 11:22

I pray for my wife the righteousness of You, God, which is through faith in Jesus Christ on she who believes.

ROMANS 3:22

———— ♥ ————

I pray, God, that in Your forbearance You have passed over my wife's sins that were previously committed.

ROMANS 3:25

———— ♥ ————

I pray that my wife will remember that if she has the gift of prophecy, and understands all mysteries and all knowledge, and though she has all faith, so that she can remove mountains, but has not love, she is nothing.

1 CORINTHIANS 13:2

———— ♥ ————

I pray that my wife will watch and that she will stand fast in the faith and that she will be brave and strong.

1 CORINTHIANS 16:13

I pray that my wife will examine herself as to whether she is in the faith and that she will test herself.

2 CORINTHIANS 13:5

♥

I pray that my wife knows that she is not justified by the works of the law but by faith in Jesus Christ.

GALATIANS 2:16

♥

I pray that my wife has been crucified with Christ. That it is no longer she who lives, but Christ who lives in her. And that the life which she now lives in the flesh she lives by faith in the Son of God, who loves her and gave Himself for her.

GALATIANS 2:20

♥

I pray that my wife knows the Holy Scriptures, which are able to make her wise

for salvation through her faith which is in
Christ Jesus.

2 TIMOTHY 3:15

———— ♥ ————

I pray that my wife will fight the good fight;
that she will finish the race; and that she
will keep the faith.

2 TIMOTHY 4:7

———— ♥ ————

I pray that the sharing of my wife's faith may
become effective by the acknowledgment
of every good thing which is in Christ Jesus.

PHILEMON 1:6

———— ♥ ————

I pray that it is by faith that my wife
understands that the worlds were framed
by the word of God, so that the things which
are seen were not made of things which are
visible.

HEBREWS 11:3

I pray that my wife will always look unto Jesus, the author and finisher of her faith, who for the joy that was set before Him endured the cross, despising the shame, and has sat down at the right hand of the throne of God.

HEBREWS 12:2

♥

I pray that my wife understands that as the body without the spirit is dead, so faith without works is dead also.

JAMES 2:26

♥

I pray that my wife will realize that if she does not believe she shall not be established.

ISAIAH 7:9

17

FEAR

God, I pray Your word to You now to remove any and all fears that my wife may be harboring either now or in the future. I ask You to remember that my prayers are actually Your words on the subject of fear. Honor Your perfect and error-free word and remove any and all fears now and forever in my wife. Thank You, God, for hearing my prayers. In Jesus' name. Amen.

God, in accordance with Your Word...

I pray that Your truth, God, shall be my wife's shield and buckler and that she shall not be afraid.

PSALM 91:4–5

♥

I pray that no evil shall befall my wife.

PSALM 91:10

I pray that my wife will not be afraid of sudden terror, nor of trouble from the wicked when it comes. I pray that You, LORD, will be her confidence and will keep her foot from being caught.

PROVERBS 3:25–26

I pray that in righteousness my wife shall be established. She shall be far from oppression, for she shall not fear. And from terror, for it shall not come near her.

ISAIAH 54:14

I pray that in You, God, my wife has put her trust and that she will not be afraid.

PSALM 56:11

I pray that my wife knows that You, God, have not given her a spirit of fear, but of power and of love and of a sound mind.

2 TIMOTHY 1:7

I pray that my wife did not receive the spirit of bondage again to fear, but that she received the Spirit of adoption by whom she cries out, "Abba, Father."

ROMANS 8:15

———— ♥ ————

I pray that in my wife there is no fear in love; because perfect love casts out fear.

1 JOHN 4:18

———— ♥ ————

I pray that You, God, will give Your angels charge over my wife, to keep her in all her ways.

PSALM 91:11

———— ♥ ————

I pray that though my wife walks through the valley of the shadow of death, she will fear no evil; for You, God, are with her. Your rod and Your staff, they comfort her.

PSALM 23:4

I pray that if You, God, are for my wife, who can be against her? Who shall separate her from the love of Christ? Shall tribulation, or distress, or persecution, or famine, or nakedness, or peril, or sword? I pray that in all these things she is more than a conqueror through Him who loved her. For I am persuaded that neither death nor life, nor angels nor principalities nor powers, nor things present nor things to come, nor height nor depth, nor any other created thing, shall be able to separate my wife from Your love, God, which is in Christ Jesus her Lord.

ROMANS 8:31, 35, 37–39

♥

I pray that my wife will be of good courage and that You, God, shall strengthen her heart for her hope is in the LORD.

PSALM 31:24

♥

I pray that my wife receives the peace that You, Jesus, have left with her, the peace You

gave to her. Let not her heart be troubled,
neither let it be afraid.

JOHN 14:27

———— ♥ ————

I pray that You, LORD, are my wife's light and
her salvation. Whom shall she fear? Though
an army may encamp against her, her heart
shall not fear. In this she will be confident.

PSALM 27:1, 3

———— ♥ ————

I pray that You, Lord, are my wife's helper
and that she will not fear.

HEBREWS 13:6

18
FINANCIAL PROBLEMS

Heavenly Father, it is not Your will that my wife should have to contend unnecessarily with financial problems. Because I believe strongly in Your word, I present to You as my prayers for my wife Your very words on this subject. Please honor Your word and release her from any and all financial problems in her life. I pray Your words in Jesus' name. Amen.

God, in accordance
with Your Word...

I pray that my wife may prosper in all things and be in health, just as her soul prospers.

3 JOHN 1:2

———— ♥ ————

I pray that You, LORD, are my wife's shepherd and that she shall not want.

PSALM 23:1

I pray that my wife will seek You, Lord, and not lack any good thing.

PSALM 34:10

———— ♥ ————

I pray that all these blessings shall come upon my wife and overtake her, because she obeys the voice of the Lord her God. She shall be blessed in the city and she shall be blessed in the country. She shall be blessed when she comes in and she shall be blessed when she goes out. I pray that You, Lord, will command Your blessing on her in her storehouses and in all to which she sets her hand.

DEUTERONOMY 28:2–3, 6–8

———— ♥ ————

I pray that my wife will give, and it will be given to her: good measure, pressed down, shaken together, and running over will be put into her bosom. For with the same measure that she uses, it will be measured back to her.

LUKE 6:38

I pray that because freely my wife has received, freely she will give.

MATTHEW 10:8

♥

I pray that on the first day of the week my wife will lay something aside, storing up as she may prosper, so that she may give to those in need.

1 CORINTHIANS 16:2

♥

I pray that my wife will bring all her tithes into the storehouse, that there may be food in God's house. And that she will try You, God, in this and see if You will not open for her the windows of heaven and pour out for her such blessing that there will not be room enough to receive it.

MALACHI 3:10

♥

I pray that my wife realizes that if she sows sparingly she will also reap sparingly and if she sows bountifully she will also reap bountifully. I pray that she will give as she purposes in her heart, not grudgingly or of necessity; for You, God, love a cheerful giver. And You are able to make all grace abound toward her, that my wife, always having all sufficiency in all things, may have an abundance for every good work.

2 CORINTHIANS 9:6–8

♥

I pray that my wife will remember that everyone who has left houses or brothers or sisters or father or mother or children or lands, for Your name's sake, Lord, shall receive a hundredfold, and inherit eternal life. I pray also that she will remember that many who are first will be last and the last first.

MATTHEW 19:29–30

♥

I pray that this Book of the Law shall not depart from my wife's mouth, but she shall meditate in it day and night, that she may observe to do according to all that is written in it. For then she will make her way prosperous, and then she will have good success.

JOSHUA 1:8

———— ♥ ————

I pray, God, that You will give wisdom and knowledge and joy to my wife who is good in Your sight. But to the sinner You will give the work of gathering and collecting, that he may give to my wife who is good before You.

ECCLESIASTES 2:26

———— ♥ ————

I pray that my wife leaves an inheritance to her children's children.

PROVERBS 13:22

———— ♥ ————

I pray that my wife does not worry, saying, "What shall I eat?" or "What shall I drink?" or "What shall I wear?" For You, her

Heavenly Father, know that she needs all these things. But I pray that she will seek first Your kingdom, God, and Your righteousness, and all these things shall be added to her. I also pray that she does not worry about tomorrow, for tomorrow will worry about its own things.

MATTHEW 6:25, 33–34

♥

I pray that You, God, shall supply all my wife's needs according to Your riches in glory by Christ Jesus.

PHILIPPIANS 4:19

19

FORGIVENESS

Lord God, for reasons known to You, my wife needs Your forgiveness. Because I sense that and know that she has need of Your forgiveness, I come to You today. I pray Your very words back to You in order that she might be forgiven. Bless now Your words on my wife's behalf. Thank You now, in Jesus' name. Amen.

God, in accordance with Your Word...

I pray that as far as the east is from the west, so far have You, God, removed my wife's transgressions from her.

PSALM 103:12

———— ♥ ————

I pray, God, that it is You who blot out my wife's transgressions for Your own sake and that You will not remember her sins.

ISAIAH 43:25

I pray that my wife will return to You, LORD,
and that You will have mercy on her; and
to her God, for You will abundantly pardon.

ISAIAH 55:7

———————— ♥ ————————

I pray that You, God, will cleanse my wife
from all her iniquity by which she has sinned
against You, and that You will pardon all her
iniquities by which she has sinned and by
which she has transgressed against You.

JEREMIAH 33:8

———————— ♥ ————————

I pray that my wife's transgressions are
forgiven and her sin is covered.

PSALM 32:1

———————— ♥ ————————

I pray that whenever my wife stands praying,
if she has anything against anyone, that she
will forgive them, so that You, her Father
in heaven, may also forgive her of her
trespasses.

MARK 11:25

I pray that in You, Jesus, my wife has redemption through Your blood, the forgiveness of her sins, according to the riches of God's grace which He made to abound toward her in all wisdom and prudence, having made known to her the mystery of His will, according to His good pleasure which He purposed in Himself.

EPHESIANS 1:7–9

♥

I pray that my wife will bear with others, and forgive others, if she has a complaint against any others, even as Christ forgave her, so she also must do.

COLOSSIANS 3:13

♥

I pray that because my wife is in Christ, she is a new creation. The old things have passed away and all things have become new.

2 CORINTHIANS 5:17

I pray that if my wife confesses her sins, that You, God, are faithful and just to forgive her sins and to cleanse her from all unrighteousness.

1 JOHN 1:9

———————— ♥ ————————

I pray that if my wife sins, she has an Advocate with You, the Father, Jesus Christ the righteous.

1 JOHN 2:1

20

GODLY LIFE

Lord Jesus, my Lord and my Savior, more than anything else I desire that my wonderful wife will live a godly life. Your words are my prayers. Please honor them by keeping my wife in the center of Your will in all that she does. Thank You for honoring this my prayer. Amen.

God, in accordance with Your Word...

I pray that if my wife lives, she lives to You, Lord; and if she dies, she dies to You, Lord. Therefore, whether she lives or dies, she is Yours, Lord.

ROMANS 14:8

———— ♥ ————

I pray that if my wife believes on You, Jesus, who justifies the ungodly, her faith is accounted for righteousness.

ROMANS 4:5

I pray that what the law could not do in my wife in that it was weak through the flesh, You, God, did by sending Your own Son in the likeness of sinful flesh, on account of sin: You condemned sin in my wife, that the righteous requirement of the law might be fulfilled in her who does not walk according to the flesh but according to the Spirit.

ROMANS 8:3–4

———————— ♥ ————————

I pray that my wife does not present her members as instruments of unrighteousness to sin, but presents herself to You, God, as being alive from the dead, and her members as instruments of righteousness to You. For sin shall not have dominion over her, for she is not under law but under grace.

ROMANS 6:13–14

———————— ♥ ————————

I pray that my wife will present her body as a living sacrifice, holy, and acceptable to You, God.

ROMANS 12:1

I pray that my wife will not be conformed
to this world, but that she will be
transformed by the renewing of her mind,
that she may prove what is that good and
acceptable and perfect will of God.

ROMANS 12:2

♥

I pray that my wife will not think of herself
more highly than she ought to think, but
to think soberly, as You, God, have dealt to
her a measure of faith.

ROMANS 12:3

♥

I pray that because You, Christ, are in my
wife, her body is dead because of sin, but
the Spirit is life because of righteousness.

ROMANS 8:10

♥

I pray that my wife whom You, God,
predestined, You also called; she whom You

called, You also justified; and she whom You
justified, You also glorified.

ROMANS 8:30

I pray that because my wife is in You, Christ,
she is a new creation; old things have passed
away, behold, all things have become new.

2 CORINTHIANS 5:17

I pray that You, God, made Jesus who knew
no sin to be sin for my wife, that she might
become the righteousness of You in Him.

2 CORINTHIANS 5:21

I pray that You, God, are able to make all
grace abound toward my wife, that she,
always having all sufficiency in all things,
may have an abundance for every good work.

2 CORINTHIANS 9:8

I pray that my wife will remember that her body is the temple of the Holy Spirit who is in her, whom she has from You, God. And that she is not her own for it was bought at a price. Therefore, I pray that she will glorify God in her body and in her spirit, which are Yours, God.

1 CORINTHIANS 6:19–20

♥

I pray that if my wife glories, she will glory in You, LORD.

1 CORINTHIANS 1:31

♥

I pray that my wife will not let sin reign in her mortal body, that she should obey it in its lusts.

ROMANS 6:12

♥

I pray that my wife has been set free from sin and has become a slave of God.

ROMANS 6:22

I pray that my wife will be renewed in the spirit of her mind and that she will put on her new self which was created according to You, God, in true righteousness and holiness.

EPHESIANS 4:23–24

♥

I pray that it is good for my wife to draw near to You, God; to put her trust in the Lord GOD, that she may declare all Your works.

PSALM 73:28

♥

I pray that my wife will delight herself in You, LORD, and that You shall give her the desires of her heart.

PSALM 37:4

♥

I pray that You, God, will satisfy my wife's mouth with good things so that her youth is renewed like the eagle's.

PSALM 103:5

I pray that You, God, are a companion to my wife who fears You and keeps Your precepts.

PSALM 119:63

♥

I pray that my wife, who walks in the law of the LORD, will be blessed.

PSALM 119:1

♥

I pray that my wife's ways are directed to keep Your statutes, God.

PSALM 119:5

♥

I pray that with my wife's whole heart she has sought You, God. Let her not wander from Your commandments.

PSALM 119:10

I pray that my wife will cleanse her way by
taking heed according to Your word, God.

PSALM 119:9

———— ♥ ————

I pray that my wife has hidden Your word
in her heart, God, that she might not sin
against You.

PSALM 119:11

———— ♥ ————

I pray that my wife will delight herself in
Your statutes, God, and that she will not
forget Your word.

PSALM 119:16

———— ♥ ————

I pray that You, God, will open my wife's
eyes, that she may see wondrous things from
Your law.

PSALM 119:18

I pray, God, that Your testimonies also are my wife's delight and her counselors.

PSALM 119:24

———————— ♥ ————————

I pray that my wife has declared her ways and that You, God, have answered her and that You will teach her Your statutes.

PSALM 119:26

———————— ♥ ————————

I pray that You, God, will make my wife understand the way of Your precepts; so shall she meditate on Your wondrous works.

PSALM 119:27

———————— ♥ ————————

I pray that my wife has chosen the way of truth and that Your judgments she has laid before her. I pray that she will cling to Your testimonies, God, and that she will not be put to shame.

PSALM 119:30–31

I pray, God, that You will make my wife walk in the path of Your commandments and that she will delight in it.

PSALM 119:35

------------ ♥ ------------

I pray that my wife will incline her heart to Your testimonies, God, and not to covetousness. I pray that she will turn away her eyes from looking at worthless things and that You will revive her in Your way.

PSALM 119:36–37

------------ ♥ ------------

I pray that You, God, will remember the word to my wife, Your servant, upon which You have caused her to hope.

PSALM 119:49

------------ ♥ ------------

I pray that You, God, will be merciful to my wife according to Your word.

PSALM 119:58

I pray, O God, that my wife has thought about her ways and has turned her feet to Your testimonies. I pray that she has made haste, and did not delay to keep Your commandments.

PSALM 119:59–60

♥

I pray that You, God, will teach my wife good judgment and knowledge, for she believes Your commandments.

PSALM 119:66

♥

I pray, God, that Your hands have made my wife and fashioned her. Give her understanding that she may learn Your commandments.

PSALM 119:73

♥

I pray, God, that You will let Your merciful kindness be for my wife's comfort.

PSALM 119:73

I pray, God, that You will let my wife's heart
be blameless regarding Your statutes, that
she may not be ashamed.

PSALM 119:80

———— ♥ ————

I pray, Lord God, that my wife will never
forget Your precepts, for by them You have
given her life.

PSALM 119:93

———— ♥ ————

I pray that Your Word, O God, is a lamp to
my wife's feet and a light to her path.

PSALM 119:105

———— ♥ ————

I pray that You, God, are my wife's hiding
place and her shield and that her hope is
in Your word.

PSALM 119:114

I pray that You, God, will give my wife understanding that she may know Your testimonies.

PSALM 119:125

———— ♥ ————

I pray that my wife's steps are directed by Your word, God, and that You let no iniquity have dominion over her.

PSALM 119:133

———— ♥ ————

I pray that my wife shall love You, the LORD her God, with all her heart, with all her soul, with all her mind, and with all her strength and that she shall love her neighbor as herself.

MARK 12:30–31

———— ♥ ————

I pray that You, Jesus, are always at my wife's right hand, that she may not be shaken.

ACTS 2:25

I pray that my wife may gain You, Christ, and be found in You, not having her own righteousness, which is from the law, but that which is through faith in You, the righteousness which is from God by faith; that she may know You and the power of Your resurrection, and the fellowship of Your sufferings, being conformed to Your death.

PHILIPPIANS 3:8–10

———— ♥ ————

I pray that if my wife confesses her sins, that You, God, are faithful and just to forgive her sins and to cleanse her from all unrighteousness.

1 JOHN 1:9

———— ♥ ————

I pray that the work of my wife's righteousness will be peace, and the effect of her righteousness, quietness and assurance forever.

ISAIAH 32:17

I pray that blessed is my wife who walks not
in the counsel of the ungodly, nor stands
in the path of sinners, nor sits in the seat
of the scornful. But her delight is in the law
of the LORD, and in Your law she meditates
day and night. I pray that she shall be like
a tree planted by the rivers of water that
brings forth its fruit in its season, whose leaf
also shall not wither; and whatever she does
shall prosper.

PSALM 1:1–3

━━━━━━━━━ ♥ ━━━━━━━━━

I pray that my wife shall know the truth and
the truth shall make her free.

JOHN 8:32

━━━━━━━━━ ♥ ━━━━━━━━━

I pray that my wife takes up Your whole
armor, God, that she may be able to
withstand in the evil day, and having done
all, to stand. I pray that she will gird her waist
with truth, that she will put on the breastplate
of righteousness and will shoe her feet with
the preparation of the gospel of peace and

above all, take the shield of faith with which
she will be able to quench all the fiery darts
of the wicked one. I pray that she will take
the helmet of salvation, and the sword of
the Spirit, which is the word of God; praying
always with all prayer and supplication in
the Spirit, being watchful to this end with
all perseverance and supplication for all the
saints.

EPHESIANS 6:13–18

———— ♥ ————

I pray that my wife will be diligent to present
herself approved to You, God, a worker who
does not need to be ashamed, rightly
dividing the word of truth.

2 TIMOTHY 2:15

———— ♥ ————

I pray that my wife will not be deceived for
You, God, are not mocked; for whatever she
sows, that she will also reap.

GALATIANS 6:7

I pray that no one deceives my wife with empty words.

EPHESIANS 5:6

♥

I pray that my wife will be a doer of the word and not a hearer only.

JAMES 1:22

♥

I pray that my wife always remembers that all Scripture is given by inspiration of You, God, and is profitable for doctrine, for reproof, for correction, for instruction in righteousness, that the man of God may be complete, thoroughly equipped for every good work.

2 TIMOTHY 3:16–17

21

GOD'S LOVE

Lord God, I pray Your words as my way to ask You to love my wife in a very special way. Help her, Lord, to experience Your love through Your word. Thank You, Father, in Jesus' name. Amen.

God, in accordance with Your Word...

I pray that my wife knows that love is not that she loved You, God, but that You loved her and sent Your Son to be the propitiation for her sins.

1 JOHN 4:10

♥

I pray that my wife loves You, God, because You first loved her.

1 JOHN 4:19

I pray that You, Christ, may dwell in my
wife's heart through faith and that she, being
rooted and grounded in love, may be able
to comprehend with all the saints what is
the width and length and depth and
height—to know Your love which passes
knowledge; that she may be filled with all
the fullness of God.

EPHESIANS 3:17–19

———— ♥ ————

I pray that my wife never forgets that You,
God, demonstrated Your own love toward
her, in that while she was still a sinner, Christ
died for her.

ROMANS 5:8

———— ♥ ————

I pray that neither death nor life, nor angels
nor principalities nor powers, nor things
present nor things to come, nor height nor
depth, nor any other created thing, shall be

able to separate my wife from the love of
You, God, which is in Christ Jesus her Lord.

ROMANS 8:38–39

———————— ♥ ————————

I pray that You, God, so loved my wife that
You gave Your only begotten Son, that my
wife who believes in Him should not perish
but have everlasting life.

JOHN 3:16

———————— ♥ ————————

I pray that my wife has Your commandments,
Jesus, and keeps them and loves You. And
because she loves You will be loved by God,
and You will love her and manifest Yourself
to her.

JOHN 14:21

———————— ♥ ————————

I pray that my wife knows that You, God,
have loved her with an everlasting love and
with lovingkindness You have drawn her.

JEREMIAH 31:3

I pray that my wife realizes that You, God, will rejoice over her with gladness. That You will quiet her in your love and that You will rejoice over her with singing.

ZEPHANIAH 3:17

22

GOD'S WORD

Heavenly Father, Your word is such an important part of my life. I pray that it will be the same in my wife's life and that Your word will be sharper than any two-edged sword in her life. I pray for Your word to be important to her. Thank You, Father, in Jesus' name for hearing and answering my prayers. Amen.

God, in accordance with Your Word...

I pray, God, that in my wife's life Your word is living and powerful, and sharper than any two-edged sword, piercing even to the division of her soul, spirit, and of her joints and marrow, and that it is a discerner of the thoughts and intents of her heart.

HEBREWS 4:12

I pray that my wife has been born again,
not of corruptible seed but incorruptible,
through Your word, God, which lives and
abides forever.

1 PETER 1:23

———— ♥ ————

I pray that my wife never forgets that the
word of the LORD endures forever.

1 PETER 1:25

———— ♥ ————

I pray that my wife puts into practice the
fact that she shall not live by bread alone,
but by every word that proceeds from the
mouth of God.

MATTHEW 4:4

———— ♥ ————

I pray that my wife will always understand
and apply the fact that all Scripture is given
by Your inspiration, God, and is profitable
for doctrine, for reproof, for correction, for

instruction in righteousness, that she may
be complete, thoroughly equipped for every
good work.

2 TIMOTHY 3:16–17

———— ♥ ————

I pray that my wife knows that she has been
given exceedingly great and precious
promises, that through these she may be a
partaker of the divine nature, having escaped
the corruption that is in the world through
lust.

2 PETER 1:4

———— ♥ ————

I pray that my wife always remembers that
heaven and earth will pass away, but Jesus'
words will by no means pass away.

MATTHEW 24:35

———— ♥ ————

I pray that my wife understands the
significance of the fact that until heaven and
earth pass away, one jot or one tittle will

by no means pass from the law till all is
fulfilled.

MATTHEW 5:18

❤

I pray that my wife takes to heart the fact
that heaven and earth will pass away, but
Your words, Jesus, will by no means pass
away.

MARK 13:31

❤

I pray that if my wife will abide in Your
words, Jesus, she is Your disciple indeed. And
if she does that she shall know the truth and
the truth shall make her free.

JOHN 8:31–32

❤

I pray that my wife's walk with You, Lord,
will be so close that her ears shall hear a
word behind her, saying, "This is the way,
walk in it."

ISAIAH 30:21

I pray that my wife realizes the significance of the fact that You, God, said, "So shall My word be that goes forth from My mouth; it shall not return to Me void."

ISAIAH 55:11

♥

I pray that You, O God, will instruct my wife and teach her in the way she should go and that You will guide her with Your eye.

PSALM 32:8

♥

I pray that my wife will remember that Your word is a lamp to her feet and a light to her path.

PSALM 119:105

♥

I pray that my wife will give attention to Your words; O God, that she will incline her ear to Your sayings. Do not let them depart from her eyes and keep them in the midst of her heart, for they are life to her when she finds them and health to her flesh.

PROVERBS 4:20–22

———— ♥ ————

I pray, O God, that my wife will take Your testimonies as a heritage forever, for they are the rejoicing of her heart.

PSALM 119:111

———— ♥ ————

I pray that my wife is Your servant, O God, and that You will give her understanding that she may know Your testimonies.

PSALM 119:125

———— ♥ ————

I pray, God, that my wife will know that every word of God is pure and that You are a shield to those who put their trust in You. I pray that she will not add to Your words, lest You rebuke her, and she be found a liar.

PROVERBS 30:5–6

I pray, God, that my wife will not let Your
Book of the Law depart from her mouth,
but she shall meditate in it day and night,
that she may observe to do according to
all that is written in it. For then she will make
her way prosperous, and then she will have
good success.

JOSHUA 1:8

23

GRIEF / HURTING

God, You know the hurt in my wife's life. And You already know other hurts that are yet to come to her. By and through Your word I pray that You will console my wife in a special way. Wipe away her tears and bring joy back into her life. I pray Your own words for those results. Please hear and honor them in Jesus' name. Amen.

God, in accordance with Your Word...

I pray that You, God, will comfort my wife who mourns and give her beauty for ashes, the oil of joy for mourning, the garment of praise for the spirit of heaviness so that she may be called a tree of righteousness.

ISAIAH 61:2–3

------ ♥ ------

I pray, O God, that You will comfort my wife in all her tribulations, that she may be able

to comfort those who are in any trouble,
with the comfort with which she herself is
comforted by You.

2 CORINTHIANS 1:4

♥

I pray that my wife is blessed when she
mourns for she shall be comforted.

MATTHEW 5:4

♥

I pray that my wife will not be ignorant
concerning those who have fallen asleep,
lest she sorrow as others who have no hope.

1 THESSALONIANS 4:13

♥

I pray that when my wife passes through
the waters, You, God, will be with her and
through the rivers, they shall not overflow
her. When she walks through the fire, she
shall not be burned, nor shall the flame
scorch her.

ISAIAH 43:2

I pray, O God, that You have comforted my
wife and will have mercy on her affliction.

ISAIAH 49:13

♥

I pray that the Lord Jesus Christ Himself and
You, God, who have loved my wife and
given her everlasting consolation and good
hope by grace, will comfort her heart and
establish her in every good word and work.

2 THESSALONIANS 2:16–17

♥

I pray that my wife always remembers that
in You, Jesus, she does not have a High
Priest who cannot sympathize with her
weaknesses, but was in all points tempted
as she is, yet without sin. Let her therefore
come boldly to the throne of grace, that she
may obtain mercy and find grace to help
in time of need.

HEBREWS 4:15–16

I pray that though my wife may walk
through the valley of the shadow of death,
she will fear no evil; for You, God, are with
her and Your rod and Your staff, they
comfort her.

PSALM 23:4

———— ♥ ————

I pray that in this crucial time in my wife's
life she can say, "O Death, where is your
sting? O Hades, where is your victory?"

1 CORINTHIANS 15:55

———— ♥ ————

I pray that this is my wife's comfort in her
affliction, that Your word has given her life.

PSALM 119:50

———— ♥ ————

I pray that my wife will cast all her cares
upon You, O God, for You care for her.

1 PETER 5:7

I pray that You, God, will wipe away every tear from my wife's eyes and that there shall be no more death, nor sorrow, nor crying. I pray that there shall be no more pain, for the former things have passed away.

REVELATION 21:4

♥

I pray that my wife will fear not, for You, God, are with her. I pray that she will not be dismayed, for You are her God. I pray that You will strengthen her and help her and that You will uphold her with Your righteous right hand.

ISAIAH 41:10

♥

I pray that my wife will walk by faith and not by sight and that she is confident, yes, well pleased rather to be absent from the body and to be present with You, Lord.

2 CORINTHIANS 5:7–8

I pray that my wife shall obtain joy and gladness and that sorrow and sighing shall flee away.

ISAIAH 51:11

24

INHERITANCE

Lord God, in Your Son's name and through Your
perfect word, I pray that my wife will be fully aware
of and never forget the magnitude of the inheritance
that awaits her. Give her a vision of that inheritance
as I pray Your words for her. Thank You, God, in
Jesus' name. Amen.

God, in accordance
with Your Word...

I pray that whatever my wife does, she will
do it heartily, as to You, Lord, and not to
men, knowing that from You she will receive
the reward of the inheritance; for she serves
the Lord Christ.

COLOSSIANS 3:23–24

———— ♥ ————

I pray that my wife has been given
exceedingly great and precious promises,
that through these she may be a partaker

of the divine nature, having escaped the
corruption that is in the world through lust.

2 PETER 1:4

———— ♥ ————

I pray that my wife has an inheritance
incorruptible and undefiled and that does
not fade away, reserved in heaven for her.

1 PETER 1:4

———— ♥ ————

I commend my wife to You, God, and to
the word of Your grace, which is able to
build her up and give her an inheritance
among all those who are sanctified.

ACTS 20:32

———— ♥ ————

I pray, God, that the Spirit Himself bears
witness with my spirit that my wife is a child
of Yours and if a child, then an heir—an heir
of Yours and a joint heir with Christ, if indeed

she suffers with Him, that she may also be
glorified together with Him.

ROMANS 8:16–17

———— ♥ ————

I pray that my wife in You, Jesus, has
obtained an inheritance, being predestined
according to the purpose of Him who works
all things according to the counsel of His
will, that she who first trusted in You should
be to the praise of His glory. In You, Jesus,
she also trusted, after you heard the word
of truth, the gospel of her salvation; in whom
also, having believed, she was sealed with
the Holy Spirit of promise, who is the
guarantee of our inheritance until the
redemption of the purchased possession, to
the praise of His glory.

EPHESIANS 1:11–14

———— ♥ ————

I pray, Lord, that my wife is aware that eye
has not seen, nor ear heard, nor have

entered into her heart the things which You have prepared for those who love You.

1 CORINTHIANS 2:9

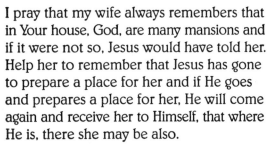

I pray that my wife always remembers that in Your house, God, are many mansions and if it were not so, Jesus would have told her. Help her to remember that Jesus has gone to prepare a place for her and if He goes and prepares a place for her, He will come again and receive her to Himself, that where He is, there she may be also.

JOHN 14:2–3

25

LONELY

Jesus, I pray to You concerning any feeling of being lonely that my wife may be experiencing now or may experience in the future. As I pray Your words, help her to remember that You said You would be with her always and that You are her constant companion. I pray Your very words to this end. In Your name I pray. Amen.

God, in accordance with Your Word...

I pray that my wife remembers Jesus' promise to be with her always, even to the end of the age.

MATTHEW 28:20

I pray that my wife's conduct will be without covetousness, and that she will be content

with such things as she has. For You, God,
said, "I will never leave you nor forsake you."

HEBREWS 13:5

———— ♥ ————

I pray that my wife will fear not, for You,
God, are with her. That she be not dismayed,
for You are her God. I pray that You will
strengthen her and that You will help her
and that You will uphold her with Your
righteous right hand.

ISAIAH 41:10

———— ♥ ————

I pray that my wife realizes that You, God,
count the number of the stars and call them
all by name. I pray that she remembers that
great is her Lord and mighty in power and
that Your understanding is infinite.

PSALM 147:4–5

———— ♥ ————

I pray, God, that neither death nor life, nor
angels nor principalities nor powers, nor

things present nor things to come, nor height
nor depth, nor any other created thing, shall
be able to separate my wife from Your love,
God, which is in Christ Jesus her Lord.

ROMANS 8:38–39

———— ♥ ————

I pray, Jesus, that my wife remembers Your
promise that You will not leave her as an
orphan but that You will come to her.

JOHN 14:18

———— ♥ ————

I pray that if my wife's father and her mother
forsake her, then You, LORD, will take care
of her.

PSALM 27:10

———— ♥ ————

I pray that my wife will be strong and of
good courage and that she does not fear
nor is she afraid, for You, the LORD her God,

are the One who goes with her. I pray that
You will not leave her nor forsake her.

DEUTERONOMY 31:6

♥

I pray that though the mountains shall depart
and the hills be removed, Your kindness,
God, shall not depart from my wife, nor shall
Your covenant of peace be removed from
her.

ISAIAH 54:10

♥

I pray, O God, that You are my wife's refuge
and strength and a very present help in
trouble.

PSALM 46:1

26

LOVE

God, Your word tells us that You are love and that we must love others even as You have loved us. This is such an important matter that I want now to pray Your very words on this subject to You on my wife's behalf. Honor Your words, Lord, as my prayers for my wife. Thank You for the privilege of praying in Jesus' name. Amen.

God, in accordance with Your Word...

I pray that my wife will love others, for love is of You, God.

1 JOHN 4:7

❤

I pray that my wife understands the true meaning of love and that though she speaks with the tongues of men and of angels, but has not love, she has become sounding brass

or a clanging cymbal. And though she has
the gift of prophecy, and understands all
mysteries and all knowledge, and though
she has all faith, so that she can remove
mountains, but has not love, she is nothing.
And though she bestows all her goods to
feed the poor, and though she gives her body
to be burned, but has not love, it profits her
nothing. I pray that she remembers that love
suffers long and is kind; love does not envy;
love does not parade itself, is not puffed up;
does not behave rudely, does not seek its
own, is not provoked, thinks no evil; does
not rejoice in iniquity, but rejoices in the
truth; bears all things, believes all things,
hopes all things, endures all things. Help her
to understand that love never fails. Help her
to abide in faith, hope, love, these three; but
the greatest of these is love.

1 CORINTHIANS 13:1–8, 13

♥

I pray that my wife understands that love
is not that she loved You, God, but that You
loved her and sent Your Son to be the
propitiation for her sins. And help her to

know that if You so loved her, she also ought
to love others.

1 JOHN 4:10–11

———— ♥ ————

I pray that my wife totally understands that
as You, God, loved Jesus, He also loves her
and she is to abide in His love.

JOHN 15:9

———— ♥ ————

I pray that if my wife has Jesus'
commandments and keeps them, it is she
who loves Him. And my wife who loves Jesus
will be loved by You, God, and Jesus will
love her and manifest Himself to her.

JOHN 14:21

———— ♥ ————

I pray that You, God, will bring to my wife's
mind that it is Jesus' commandment that she
love others just as He has loved her.

JOHN 15:12

I pray that my wife has known and believed
the love that You, God, have for her and
that she who loves You must love her
brother also.

1 JOHN 4:16, 21

———— ♥ ————

I pray, God, that You have loved my wife with
an everlasting love and with lovingkindness
have drawn her to You.

JEREMIAH 31:3

———— ♥ ————

I pray that You, God, love my wife, because
she has loved Jesus, and has believed that
He came forth from You.

JOHN 16:27

———— ♥ ————

I pray that my wife will realize that You, God,
demonstrated Your own love toward her in
that while she was still a sinner, Christ died
for her.

ROMANS 5:8

I pray that my wife shall love You, the LORD her God, with all her heart, with all her soul, with all her mind, and with all her strength and that she shall love her neighbor as herself.

MARK 12:30–31

♥

I pray that You, God, so loved my wife that You gave Your only begotten Son, that she who believes in Him should not perish but have everlasting life.

JOHN 3:16

♥

I pray that neither death nor life, nor angels nor principalities nor powers, nor things present nor things to come, nor height nor depth, nor any other created thing, shall be able to separate my wife from Your love, God, which is in Christ Jesus her Lord.

ROMANS 8:38–39

I pray, Jesus, that my wife will take heed to the new commandment You gave to her that she love others as You have loved her and that by this she will know that she is Your disciple, if she has love for others.

JOHN 13:34–35

27

LOVE FOR MY WIFE

Lord, I pray Your words for my wife. Honor my prayers by honoring Your own words. I praise You and pray to You in Jesus' name. Amen.

God, in accordance with Your Word...

I pray that while my wife and I have not seen You, God, at any time, if we love one another, You abide in us, and Your love has been perfected in us.

1 JOHN 4:12

♥

I pray, Jesus, that my wife and I will follow Your commandment that we love one another as You have loved us.

JOHN 15:12

I pray that if You, God, so loved my wife
and me, we also ought to love one another.

1 JOHN 4:11

♥

I pray, Lord Jesus, that by this my wife and
I know love, because You laid down Your
life for us. And we also ought to lay down
our lives for each other.

1 JOHN 3:16

♥

I pray, Lord God, that my wife and I will love
one another, for love is of You; and everyone
who loves is born of You and knows You.
But if we do not love we do not know You,
for You are love.

1 JOHN 4:7–8

♥

I pray, Jesus, that my wife and I will follow
Your command that we love one another.

JOHN 15:17

I pray that my wife and I may with one mind and one mouth glorify the God and Father of our Lord Jesus Christ.

ROMANS 15:6

♥

I pray that my wife and I will always understand the significance of the question, "Can two walk together, unless they are agreed?"

AMOS 3:3

28

MARITAL PROBLEMS

Lord God, I ask You to honor Your word in this very sensitive area and to be with my wife in every way possible. I love You, and I love my wife. Be with her now, and in Jesus' name I ask You to bless the praying of Your word at all times. Thank You for hearing my prayers. Amen.

God, in accordance with Your Word...

I pray that as for my wife and my house, we will serve You, LORD.

JOSHUA 24:15

———— ♥ ————

I pray that my wife will be submissive to me, her husband.

1 PETER 3:1

I pray that just as the church is subject to Christ, so will my wife be to me in everything.

EPHESIANS 5:24

—————— ♥ ——————

I pray that my wife has read that You, the LORD God, said, "It is not good that man should be alone; I will make her a helper comparable to him."

GENESIS 2:18

—————— ♥ ——————

I pray that my wife always understands that a man shall leave his father and mother and be joined to his wife, and they shall become one flesh.

GENESIS 2:24

—————— ♥ ——————

I pray, God, that my wife and I will let all bitterness, wrath, anger, clamor, and evil speaking be put away from us, with all malice. And that we will be kind to one another, tenderhearted, forgiving one another, just as You, God, in Christ forgave us.

EPHESIANS 4:31–32

♥

I pray that my wife will behave wisely in a perfect way and that she will walk within our house with a perfect heart.

PSALM 101:2

♥

I pray that my wife and I will be of one mind, having compassion for one another, that we will be tenderhearted and courteous, not returning evil for evil or reviling for reviling, but on the contrary blessing, knowing that we were called to this, that we may inherit a blessing.

1 PETER 3:8–9

♥

I pray that my wife and I will trust in You, LORD, with all our hearts and lean not on

our own understanding and that in all our
ways we will acknowledge You, O God, and
that You shall direct our paths.

PROVERBS 3:5–6

———— ♥ ————

I pray that my wife and I remember that
hatred stirs up strife but love covers all sins.

PROVERBS 10:12

———— ♥ ————

I pray that since my wife and I have purified
our souls in obeying the truth through the
Spirit in sincere love of each other, that we
will love one another fervently with a pure
heart.

1 PETER 1:22

29

MARRIAGE

Holy Father, You have given us marriage as something sacred. It is important to You, and it is important to us. Hear now Your words as my prayers and honor them according to Your promises. I pray in Jesus' name, and I thank You. Amen.

God, in accordance with Your Word...

I pray that my wife will honor her husband.

ESTHER 1:20

— ♥ —

I pray that my wife will watch over the ways of her household and that she does not eat the bread of idleness.

PROVERBS 31:27

I pray that I will not depart from my wife.

1 CORINTHIANS 7:10

———— ♥ ————

I pray that I will love my wife.

EPHESIANS 5:25

———— ♥ ————

I pray that my wife will submit to me as to the Lord.

EPHESIANS 5:22

———— ♥ ————

I pray that my wife will love me and that she will love our children.

EPHESIANS 5:25

———— ♥ ————

I pray that as the elect of God, holy and beloved, that my wife and I put on tender mercies, kindness, humility, meekness, and longsuffering. I pray that we will bear with

one another, forgiving one another, if we
have a complaint against each other, even
as Christ forgave us, so we also must do.
But above all these things help us to put on
love, which is the bond of perfection.

COLOSSIANS 3:12–14

30

NEEDS

Lord, You and You alone know all of my wife's needs. I desire now to ask You to bless and honor the praying of Your word by meeting my wife's needs as only You can do. I pray in Jesus' name. Amen.

God, in accordance with Your Word...

I pray that my wife will delight herself also in You, LORD, and that You will give her the desires of her heart.

PSALM 37:4

♥

I pray that You, God, will open Your hand and satisfy the desire of my wife.

PSALM 145:16

I pray that You, Lord, will guide my wife
continually.

ISAIAH 58:11

———— ♥ ————

I pray that my wife will not spend wages
for what does not satisfy and that she will
listen carefully to You, God, and will let her
soul delight itself in abundance.

ISAIAH 55:2

———— ♥ ————

I pray that whatever things my wife asks for
in prayer, believing, she will receive.

MATTHEW 21:22

———— ♥ ————

I pray, Jesus, that if my wife asks anything
in Your name You will do it.

JOHN 14:14

I pray, Lord Jesus, that if my wife abides in You and Your words abide in her, she will ask what she desires, and it shall be done for her.

JOHN 15:7

❤

I pray that my wife will ask in Your name, Jesus, and she will receive, that her joy may be full.

JOHN 16:24

❤

I pray that my wife shall know the truth and the truth shall make her free.

JOHN 8:32

❤

I pray that You, the God and Father of our Lord Jesus Christ, have blessed my wife with every spiritual blessing in the heavenly places in Christ.

EPHESIANS 1:3

I pray that my wife can do all things through Christ who strengthens her.

PHILIPPIANS 4:13

♥

I pray that You, my God, shall supply all my wife's needs according to Your riches in glory by Christ Jesus.

PHILIPPIANS 4:19

♥

I pray that if my wife's heart does not condemn her, she has confidence toward You, God, and whatever she asks she receives from You, because she keeps Your commandments and does those things that are pleasing in Your sight.

1 JOHN 3:21–22

31

OBEDIENCE

God, You have said that obedience is more important to You than is sacrifice. Because I believe that You meant what You said, I now pray back to You Your powerful words. God, in Jesus' name I ask You to help my wife be obedient to You in every way and in every situation. Having asked You for it in Jesus' name, I believe that it will happen, and I thank You in His name. Amen.

God, in accordance with Your Word...

I pray that my wife recognizes the fact that You, God, have set before her today a blessing and a curse: the blessing, if she obeys the commandments of the LORD her God, which You have commanded her today; and the curse, if she does not obey the commandments of the LORD her God, but turns aside from the way which You

command her today, to go after other gods
she has not known.

DEUTERONOMY 11:26–28

———— ♥ ————

I pray that my wife never forgets that to obey
is better than sacrifice.

1 SAMUEL 15:22

———— ♥ ————

I pray that my wife will heed Your
commandments, O God, so that her peace
will be like a river and her righteousness
like the waves of the sea.

ISAIAH 48:18

———— ♥ ————

I pray, O God, that my wife will obey Your
voice, and You will be her God, and she shall
be Your child. And that she will walk in all
the ways that You have commanded her, that
it may be well with her.

JEREMIAH 7:23

I pray, Lord Jesus, that my wife loves You
and keeps Your commandments.

JOHN 14:15

———— ♥ ————

I pray, God, that my wife knows that she
ought to obey You rather than men.

ACTS 5:29

———— ♥ ————

I pray, Jesus, that my wife will always keep
Your commandments.

1 JOHN 2:3

———— ♥ ————

I pray that my wife will learn Your statutes,
O God, and be careful to observe them. I
pray that she will be careful to do as You,
the Lord her God, have commanded her and
that she shall not turn aside to the right hand
or to the left. I pray that she will walk in all
the ways which You have commanded her,
and that you may prolong her days.

DEUTERONOMY 5:1, 32–33

I pray that my wife will walk in Your ways, God, to keep Your statutes and Your commandments, and that You will lengthen her days.

1 KINGS 3:14

———— ♥ ————

I pray that You, God, will teach my wife to do Your will, for You are her God.

PSALM 143:10

———— ♥ ————

I pray that whatever my wife does, she does it heartily, as to the Lord and not to men.

COLOSSIANS 3:23

32

PATIENCE

Lord Jesus, patience is so important but so elusive.
I pray to You now what You have already declared
in Your word, and I ask You to honor it in my wife's
life. Bless now the praying of Your word. Amen.

God, in accordance
with Your Word...

I pray that whatever things were written
before were written for my wife's learning,
that she through the patience and comfort
of the Scriptures might have hope. Now may
You, the God of patience and comfort, grant
my wife to be like-minded toward others,
according to Christ Jesus.

ROMANS 15:4–5

❤

I pray that my wife will glory in tribulations,
knowing that tribulation produces

perseverance; and perseverance, character;
and character, hope.

ROMANS 5:3–4

I pray that my wife will wait patiently for
You, LORD, and that You will incline Yourself
to her and hear her cry.

PSALM 40:1

I pray that my wife will imitate those who
through faith and patience inherit the
promises.

HEBREWS 6:12

I pray that my wife will rest in You, LORD,
and that she will wait patiently for You. I
pray that she does not fret because of him
who prospers in his way or because of the
man who brings wicked schemes to pass. I
pray that she will cease from anger, and

forsake wrath and that she does not fret—it only causes harm.

PSALM 37:7–8

———— ♥ ————

I pray that my wife does not cast away her confidence, which has great reward. For she has need of endurance, so that after she has done Your will, God, she may receive her promise.

HEBREWS 10:35-36

———— ♥ ————

I pray that my wife will not hasten in her spirit to be angry, for anger rests in the bosom of fools.

ECCLESIASTES 7:9

———— ♥ ————

I pray that since my wife is surrounded by so great a cloud of witnesses, let her lay aside every weight, and the sin which so

easily ensnares her, and let her run with
endurance the race that is set before her.

HEBREWS 12:1

———— ♥ ————

I pray that the fruit of the Spirit in my wife
is love, joy, peace, longsuffering, kindness,
goodness, faithfulness, gentleness, and
self-control.

GALATIANS 5:22–23

———— ♥ ————

I pray that my wife will wait on You, LORD,
and that she shall renew her strength. I pray
that she shall mount up with wings like
eagles and that she shall run and not be
weary and walk and not faint.

ISAIAH 40:31

———— ♥ ————

I pray that my wife will wait on You, LORD,
and that she will be of good courage. I also

pray that You will strengthen her heart and
that she will wait on You.

PSALM 27:14

———— ♥ ————

I pray that my wife will hope and wait quietly
for Your salvation, O LORD.

LAMENTATIONS 3:26

———— ♥ ————

I pray that my wife will hope for what she
does not see and eagerly wait for it with
perseverance.

ROMANS 8:25

———— ♥ ————

I pray that my wife understands that the
testing of her faith produces patience and
that she should let patience have its perfect
work, that she may be perfect and complete,
lacking nothing.

JAMES 1:3–4

I pray that my wife will be patient until Your coming, Lord. I pray that she will see how the farmer waits for the precious fruit of the earth, waiting patiently for it until it receives the early and latter rain and that she also will be patient, for Your coming is at hand.

JAMES 5:7–8

33

PEACE

～～

Heavenly Father, just as Your word says, I pray perfect peace for my wife. Nothing is more important than praying Your words of promised peace to her. I pray Your words in Jesus' name, and I thank You for hearing and answering my prayers. Amen.

God, in accordance with Your Word...

I pray, God, that You will keep my wife in perfect peace, whose mind is stayed on You, because she trusts in You.

ISAIAH 26:3

———— ♥ ————

I pray that Your kindness, God, shall not depart from my wife, nor shall Your covenant of peace be removed from her.

ISAIAH 54:10

I pray that my wife will lie down in peace,
and sleep; for You alone, O LORD, make her
dwell in safety.

PSALM 4:8

——————— ♥ ———————

I pray, O LORD, that You will give strength
to my wife and that You will bless her with
peace.

PSALM 29:11

——————— ♥ ———————

I pray that You, Jesus, have left Your peace
with my wife. I pray that her heart will not
be troubled, neither will she be afraid.

JOHN 14:27

——————— ♥ ———————

I pray that my wife who has been justified
by faith, will have peace with You, God,
through her Lord Jesus Christ.

ROMANS 5:1

I pray that Jesus Himself is my wife's peace.

EPHESIANS 2:14

I pray that my wife will be anxious for nothing, but in everything by prayer and supplication, with thanksgiving, will let her requests be made known to You, God; and Your peace which surpasses all understanding, will guard her heart and mind through Christ Jesus.

PHILIPPIANS 4:6–7

I pray, God, that the peace of God will rule in my wife's heart.

COLOSSIANS 3:15

34

POWER

Lord God, my wife is in need of Your power. That power comes only through Your word, and that is what I pray to You today. Honor the praying of Your word and bring Your power into the life of my wife. It is in the powerful name of Jesus that I offer up Your words in prayer for my wife. Thank You for hearing and answering each of these prayers. Amen.

God, in accordance
with Your Word...

I pray that my wife will take pleasure in infirmities, in reproaches, in needs, in persecutions, in distresses, for Christ's sake. For when she is weak, then she is strong.

2 CORINTHIANS 12:10

I pray that in all things my wife is more than a conqueror through Jesus who loved her.

ROMANS 8:37

I pray that my wife can do all things through Christ who strengthens her.

PHILIPPIANS 4:13

♥

I pray, Jesus, that whatever my wife asks in Your name that You will do, that the Father may be glorified in the Son.

JOHN 14:13

♥

I pray that You, God, are able to make all grace abound toward my wife, that she, always having all sufficiency in all things, may have an abundance for every good work.

2 CORINTHIANS 9:8

♥

I pray, Jesus, that Your grace is sufficient for my wife, for Your strength is made perfect in weakness.

2 CORINTHIANS 12:9

I pray that my wife will see the exceeding greatness of Your power, God, toward her who believes, according to the working of Your mighty power.

EPHESIANS 1:19

❤

I pray, O God, that You are able to do exceedingly abundantly above all that my wife asks or thinks, according to the power that works in her.

EPHESIANS 3:20

35

PRAISE

Heavenly Father, we were created to praise You.
Through the praying of Your word, I petition You to
put into my wife's heart a consistent desire to praise
You at all times. These words are my prayers in
Jesus' name. Amen.

God, in accordance
with Your Word...

I pray, LORD God, that my wife will sing
praises to You and that she will declare Your
deeds among the people.

PSALM 9:11

♥

I pray that my wife will sing to You, LORD,
as long as she lives.

PSALM 104:33

I pray that every day my wife will bless You,
God, and will praise Your name forever and
ever.

PSALM 145:2

———— ♥ ————

I pray that my wife will know that great is
the LORD, and greatly to be praised and that
Your greatness is unsearchable.

PSALM 145:3

———— ♥ ————

I pray that my wife's tongue shall speak of
Your righteousness, Lord, and of Your praise
all the day long.

PSALM 35:28

———— ♥ ————

I pray, O Lord, that You will open my wife's
lips and her mouth shall show forth Your
praise.

PSALM 51:15

I pray, O LORD, that my wife will praise You.

ISAIAH 12:1

———— ♥ ————

I pray that my wife will give You thanks, O Lord God Almighty, the One who is and who was and who is to come, because You have taken Your great power and reigned.

REVELATION 11:17

———— ♥ ————

I pray that my wife will hope continually, O God, and will praise You yet more and more.

PSALM 71:14

———— ♥ ————

I pray, God, that my wife will enter into Your gates with thanksgiving, and into Your courts with praise.

PSALM 100:4

I pray that You, LORD, are my wife's strength
and song, and that You have become her
salvation; that You are her God, and that
she will praise You.

EXODUS 15:2

───── ♥ ─────

I pray that my wife will proclaim the name
of the LORD and ascribe greatness to You,
her God.

DEUTERONOMY 32:3

───── ♥ ─────

I pray that my wife will proclaim, "The
LORD lives! Blessed be my Rock! Let God be
exalted, the Rock of my salvation!"

2 SAMUEL 22:47

───── ♥ ─────

I pray that my wife always remembers that
You, LORD, are great and greatly to be
praised.

1 CHRONICLES 16:25

I pray that my wife will bless You, Lord, at all times and that Your praise shall continually be in her mouth.

PSALM 34:1

———— ♥ ————

I pray, God, that You have put a new song in my wife's mouth—praise to her God.

PSALM 40:3

———— ♥ ————

I pray that my wife realizes that great is the Lord, and greatly to be praised.

PSALM 48:1

———— ♥ ————

I pray that my wife prays, "Blessed be the Lord, who daily loads me with benefits."

PSALM 68:19

I pray that my wife will give thanks to You,
LORD, for You are good! For Your mercy
endures forever.

PSALM 106:1

♥

I pray that You will let my wife's soul live,
O God, and it shall praise You.

PSALM 119:175

♥

I pray that my wife will praise You, God, for
she is fearfully and wonderfully made.
Marvelous are Your works, and that her soul
knows very well.

PSALM 139:14

♥

I pray that my wife's mouth shall speak the
praise of You, LORD.

PSALM 145:21

I pray that my wife will praise You, LORD!

PSALM 146:1

———— ♥ ————

I pray that my wife will praise You, God, for
Your mighty acts and that she will praise
You according to Your excellent greatness!

PSALM 150:2

———— ♥ ————

I pray that my wife will continually offer the
sacrifice of praise to You, God, that is, the
fruit of her lips, giving thanks to Your name.

HEBREWS 13:15

36

PROTECTION

❧

Lord God, honor the prayers I lift up to You for my wife's protection. They are Your words straight from Your Bible. Protect her at all times through the praying of Your word in Jesus' name. Amen.

God, in accordance with Your Word...

I pray that my wife's LORD God, who goes before her, will fight for her.

DEUTERONOMY 1:30

———— ♥ ————

I pray that if my wife will indeed obey Your voice, God, and do all that You speak, then You will be an enemy to her enemies and an adversary to her adversaries.

EXODUS 23:22

I pray that no weapon formed against my wife shall prosper and every tongue which rises against her in judgment You, God, shall condemn.

ISAIAH 54:17

———— ♥ ————

I pray that Jesus has given my wife the authority to trample on serpents and scorpions, and over all the power of the enemy, and nothing shall by any means hurt her.

LUKE 10:19

———— ♥ ————

I pray that You, Lord, are faithful, who will establish my wife and guard her from the evil one.

2 THESSALONIANS 3:3

———— ♥ ————

I pray that if God be for my wife, who can be against her?

ROMANS 8:31

37

REBELLIOUS

Lord God, through the power of Your word I pray that You will keep my wife free from a rebellious spirit or a rebellious attitude. I pray to You and I thank You in Jesus' precious name. Amen.

God, in accordance with Your Word...

I pray that my wife, by doing good, may put to silence the ignorance of foolish men.

1 PETER 2:15

———— ♥ ————

I pray that if my wife is willing and obedient she shall eat the good of the land.

ISAIAH 1:19

———— ♥ ————

I pray that my wife will gird up the loins of her mind, be sober, and rest her hope fully

upon the grace that is to be brought to her
at the revelation of Jesus Christ; as an
obedient child, not conforming herself to
the former lusts, as in her ignorance; but
as You, God, who called her are holy, she
also is to be holy in all her conduct.

1 PETER 1:13–15

I pray that my wife is aware that rebellion
is as the sin of witchcraft.

1 SAMUEL 15:23

I pray that my wife will obey those who rule
over her, and be submissive, for they watch
out for her soul, as those who must give
account.

HEBREWS 13:17

I pray that my wife will be like Jesus and
humble herself and become obedient.

PHILIPPIANS 2:8

I pray that like You, Jesus, my wife learns obedience by the things she suffers.

HEBREWS 5:8

♥

I pray, God, that my wife knows that You resist the proud, but give grace to the humble and that she will humble herself under Your mighty hand, that You, God, may exalt her in due time.

1 PETER 5:5–6

♥

I pray that my wife knows and understands that no grave trouble will overtake the righteous, but the wicked shall be filled with evil.

PROVERBS 12:21

♥

I pray that my wife will submit to You, God. That she will resist the devil and he will flee from her.

JAMES 4:7

I pray that while my wife was once darkness, now she is light in the Lord and that she will walk as a child of light.

EPHESIANS 5:8

♥

I pray that my wife will no longer walk in the futility of her mind.

EPHESIANS 4:17

♥

I pray that my wife does not let sin reign in her mortal body, that she should obey it in its lusts. I also pray that she does not present her members as instruments of unrighteousness to sin, but that she presents herself to You, God, as being alive from the dead, and her members as instruments of righteousness to God. For sin shall not have dominion over her, for she is not under law but under grace.

ROMANS 6:12–14

38

SALVATION

Lord, the most important thing in life is salvation. I pray for my wife's salvation through the powerful praying of Your Holy Word. Hear these my prayers for my wife. Honor them. And bless her with Your salvation. In Jesus' name I pray. Amen.

God, in accordance
with Your Word...

I pray that my wife will discover that Jesus said, "He who believes in Me has everlasting life."

JOHN 6:47

------- ♥ -------

I pray that my wife remembers that Jesus has come to seek and to save that which was lost.

LUKE 19:19

I pray, Lord Jesus, that my wife will come to understand what You meant when You said, "Therefore whoever confesses Me before men, him I will also confess before My Father who is in heaven."

MATTHEW 10:32

♥

I pray that if my wife will confess with her mouth the Lord Jesus and believe in her heart that God has raised Him from the dead, she will be saved. For with her heart she believes unto righteousness, and with her mouth confession is made unto salvation.

ROMANS 10:9–10

♥

I pray that You, God, so loved my wife that You gave Your only begotten Son, that if my wife believes in Him she should not perish but have everlasting life.

JOHN 3:16

I pray, God, that You did not send Your Son
into the world to condemn my wife, but that
my wife through Him might be saved.

JOHN 3:17

———————— ♥ ————————

I pray that this will be my wife's testimony:
that You, God, have given her eternal life,
and this life is in Your Son.

1 JOHN 5:11

———————— ♥ ————————

I pray that by grace my wife has been saved
through faith, and that not of herself; it is
the gift of God, not of works, lest she should
boast.

EPHESIANS 2:8–9

———————— ♥ ————————

I pray that You, God, have saved my wife
and called her with a holy calling, not
according to her works, but according to

Your own purpose and grace which was given to her in Christ Jesus before time began.

2 TIMOTHY 1:9

———— ♥ ————

I pray, God, that it is not by works of righteousness which my wife has done, but according to Your mercy You saved her, through the washing of regeneration and renewing of the Holy Spirit, whom You poured out on her abundantly through Jesus Christ her Savior.

TITUS 3:5–6

———— ♥ ————

I pray, God, that Jesus stands at the door and knocks and if my wife hears His voice and opens the door, He will come in to her and dine with her, and her with Him.

REVELATION 3:20

I pray, God, that my wife has been born again, not of corruptible seed but incorruptible, through Your word which lives and abides forever.

1 PETER 1:23

39

SATAN DEFEATED

Heavenly Father, my wife's enemy is Satan. He wants to destroy her. But, God, Your word is stronger than even Satan. I pray Your word that she will defeat every attack of Satan in her life. Thank You, God, in the powerful name of Jesus. Amen.

God, in accordance with Your Word...

I pray that my wife will be strong in You, Lord, and in the power of Your might. I pray that she will put on the whole armor of God, that she may be able to stand against the wiles of the devil. For she does not wrestle against flesh and blood, but against principalities, against powers, against the rulers of the darkness of this age, against spiritual hosts of wickedness in the heavenly places. I pray that she will take up Your whole armor, God, that she may be able to withstand in the evil day, and having done all, to stand. I pray that she has girded her waist with truth, having put on the breastplate of righteousness, and having shod her feet with the preparation of the gospel of peace, and above all, taking the shield of faith with which she will be able to quench all the fiery darts of the wicked one. I pray that she also takes the helmet of salvation, and the sword of the Spirit, which is the word of God; praying always with all prayer and supplication in the Spirit, being watchful to this end with all perseverance and supplication for all the saints.

EPHESIANS 6:10–18

❤

I pray that You, God, will open my wife's eyes, in order to turn them from darkness to light, and from the power of Satan to God, that she may receive forgiveness of sins and an inheritance among those who are sanctified by faith in Jesus.

ACTS 26:18

I pray, God, that You preserve the soul of my wife and deliver her out of the hand of the wicked.

PSALM 97:10

———— ♥ ————

I pray, God, for my wife that the Son of God was manifested, that He might destroy the works of the devil.

1 JOHN 3:8

———— ♥ ————

I pray for my wife that she puts off, concerning her former conduct, the old woman which grows corrupt according to the deceitful lusts, and be renewed in the spirit of her mind, and that she put on the new [person] which was created according to You, God, in true righteousness and holiness.

EPHESIANS 4:22–24

———— ♥ ————

I pray, Jesus, that my wife knows that You have disarmed principalities and powers, and have made a public spectacle of them, triumphing over them in it.

COLOSSIANS 2:15

♥

I pray, God, that my wife understands that even the angels who did not keep their proper domain, but left their own abode, You have reserved in everlasting chains under darkness for the judgment of the great day.

JUDE 1:6

♥

I pray that my wife is strong, and that the word of God abides in her and she has overcome the wicked one.

1 JOHN 2:14

♥

I pray that my wife will not give place to the devil.

EPHESIANS 4:27

I do not pray, God, that You should take my wife out of the world, but that You should keep her from the evil one.

JOHN 17:15

———— ♥ ————

I pray that my wife will submit to You, God, and that she will resist the devil and he will flee from her.

JAMES 4:7

———— ♥ ————

I pray that my wife will be sober and vigilant, because her adversary the devil walks about like a roaring lion, seeking whom he may devour. I pray that she will resist him, steadfast in the faith, knowing that the same sufferings are experienced by other Christians in the world.

1 PETER 5:8–9

———— ♥ ————

I pray that at this time my wife will remember that Jesus went about doing good and healing all who were oppressed by the devil, for God was with Him.

ACTS 10:38

———— ♥ ————

I pray that You, God, have delivered my wife from the power of darkness and conveyed her into the kingdom of Jesus, in whom she has redemption through His blood, the forgiveness of sins.

COLOSSIANS 1:13–14

———— ♥ ————

I pray that in all things my wife is more than a conqueror through Him who loved her.

ROMANS 8:37

———— ♥ ————

I pray, God, that the accuser of my wife, who accuses her before her God day and night, has been cast down. I pray that she overcame him by the blood of the Lamb and by the word of her testimony.

REVELATION 12:10–11

I pray that neither death nor life, nor angels nor principalities nor powers, nor things present nor things to come, nor height nor depth, nor any other created thing, shall be able to separate my wife from the love of God which is in Christ Jesus her Lord.

ROMANS 8:38–39

———— ♥ ————

I pray that while my wife is hard pressed on every side, yet not crushed; she is perplexed, but not in despair; persecuted, but not forsaken; struck down, but not destroyed—always carrying about in her body the dying of the Lord Jesus, that the life of Jesus also may be manifested in her body.

2 CORINTHIANS 4:8–10

———— ♥ ————

I pray that though my wife walks in the flesh, she does not war according to the flesh. For the weapons of her warfare are not carnal but mighty in God for pulling down strongholds, casting down arguments and

every high thing that exalts itself against the
knowledge of God, bringing every thought
into captivity to the obedience of Christ.

2 CORINTHIANS 10:3–5

———— ♥ ————

I pray that my wife has her senses exercised
to discern both good and evil.

HEBREWS 5:14

———— ♥ ————

I pray, Lord, that You will guard my wife from
the evil one.

2 THESSALONIANS 3:3

———— ♥ ————

I pray, God, that Your presence will go with
my wife forever.

EXODUS 33:14

———— ♥ ————

I pray, God, that my wife will be strong and
of good courage; that she is not afraid, nor

dismayed, for You, the Lord her God, are
with her wherever she goes.

JOSHUA 1:9

———— ♥ ————

I pray, God, that You will preserve the soul
of my wife and that You will deliver her out
of the hand of the wicked.

PSALM 97:10

———— ♥ ————

I pray, God, that You are my wife's refuge
and that You will thrust out the enemy from
before her.

DEUTERONOMY 33:27

———— ♥ ————

I pray, God, that the angel of the Lord
encamps all around my wife who fears You,
and delivers her.

PSALM 34:7

I pray that Satan will not take advantage of my wife for she is not ignorant of his devices.

2 CORINTHIANS 2:11

♥

I pray that my wife know that she does not live by bread alone, but by every word that proceeds from the mouth of You, God.

MATTHEW 4:4

♥

I pray, Lord, that my wife will drive Satan away by worshipping the Lord her God, and Him only she shall serve.

MATTHEW 4:10

♥

I pray that my wife will gird up the loins of her mind and be sober, and rest her hope fully upon the grace that is to be brought to her at the revelation of Jesus Christ; as an obedient child, not conforming herself to the former lusts, as in her ignorance; but

as You, God, who called her are holy, may
she also be holy in all her conduct.

1 PETER 1:13–15

———————— ♥ ————————

I pray that my wife will have the mind of
Christ.

1 CORINTHIANS 2:16

STARTED PRAYING THESE FOR AMY 2-5-94.
THANK YOU LORD GOD ALMIGHTY FOR SENDING
YOUR ONLY BEGTTEN SON, JESUS CHRIST, THE
LORD OF GLORY, AND KING OF KINGS ~~~~~~
FOR OUR SALVATION, AND THANK YOU GOD
FOR HEARING & HONORING THESE PRAYERS,
IN JESUS NAME I PRAY AMEN

40

SECURITY

Lord, real and true security comes only from You. I pray Your words concerning security for my wife. Through the praying of Your word, help her to sense the security that only You can give. Lord, I thank You and I pray in Your name. Amen.

God, in accordance with Your Word...

I pray that my wife is persuaded that neither death nor life, nor angels nor principalities nor powers, nor things present nor things to come, nor height nor depth, nor any other created thing, shall be able to separate her from the love of God which is in Christ Jesus her Lord.

ROMANS 8:38–39

———— ♥ ————

I pray that in Jesus my wife also trusted, after she heard the word of truth, the gospel of

her salvation; in whom also, having believed,
she was sealed with the Holy Spirit of
promise.

EPHESIANS 1:13

———— ♥ ————

I pray that surely goodness and mercy shall
follow my wife all the days of her life and
that she will dwell in the house of the LORD
forever.

PSALM 23:6

———— ♥ ————

I pray that my wife is one of those who has
come to You, Jesus, and who You will by
no means cast out.

JOHN 6:37

———— ♥ ————

I pray, Jesus, that my wife has heard Your
voice and that You know her, and that she
follows You, and that You will give her
eternal life, and she shall never perish.

JOHN 10:27–28

I pray that my wife does not grieve the Holy Spirit of God, by whom she was sealed for the day of redemption.

EPHESIANS 4:30

♥

I pray that You, God, who have begun a good work in my wife will complete it until the day of Jesus Christ.

PHILIPPIANS 1:6

♥

I pray, Lord, that Your faithfulness will establish my wife and guard her from the evil one.

2 THESSALONIANS 3:3

♥

I pray that You, God, are able to keep my wife from stumbling, and to present her faultless before the presence of Your glory with exceeding joy.

JUDE 1:24

41

SERVING GOD

Lord God, in accordance with Your perfect word I pray that my wife will walk after You and that she will serve You. Your word is clear that she cannot serve two masters. Now—at this very moment—I ask You to honor Your word in the area of my wife's service to You. Use Your Holy Spirit to guide her and direct her in this area of her life. Thank You. In Jesus' name. Amen.

God, in accordance with Your Word...

I pray that my wife will walk after You, the LORD her God, and fear You, and keep Your commandments and obey Your voice, and that she shall serve You and hold fast to You.

DEUTERONOMY 13:4

♥

I pray, God, that my wife knows that she cannot serve two masters; for either she will

hate the one and love the other, or else she
will be loyal to the one and despise the other.
She cannot serve You and mammon.

MATTHEW 6:24

———————— ♥ ————————

I pray that my wife will serve You, the Lord
her God, and You only she shall serve.

MATTHEW 4:10

———————— ♥ ————————

I pray that my wife will love you, the LORD
her God, and walk in all Your ways, keeping
Your commandments, and holding fast to
You, and will serve You with all her heart
and with all her soul.

JOSHUA 22:5

———————— ♥ ————————

I pray to You, God, that my wife will present
her body a living sacrifice, holy, acceptable
to You, which is her reasonable service. I
pray also that she will not be conformed
to this world, but be transformed by the

renewing of her mind, that she may prove
what is that good and acceptable and perfect
will of Yours, God.

ROMANS 12:1–2

♥

I pray that my wife will be kindly affectionate
to others with brotherly love, in honor
giving preference to others; not lagging in
diligence, fervent in spirit, serving You,
Lord; rejoicing in hope, patient in
tribulation, continuing steadfastly in prayer;
distributing to the needs of the saints,
given to hospitality.

ROMANS 12:10–13

♥

I pray, O God, that my wife shall serve You,
the Lord her God.

EXODUS 23:25

♥

I pray that my wife will fear You, the Lord
her God, and walk in all Your ways and love

You, and serve You, the LORD her God, with
all her heart and with all her soul and that
she will keep Your commandments and Your
statutes which You command her today for
her good.

DEUTERONOMY 10:12–13

———— ♥ ————

I pray that my wife does not turn aside from
following You, LORD, but serves You with all
her heart. I pray that she does not turn aside,
for then she would go after empty things
which cannot profit or deliver, for they are
nothing. For You will not forsake her, for
Your great name's sake, because it has
pleased You to make her Yours.

1 SAMUEL 12:20–22

———— ♥ ————

I pray that my wife will know You, God, and
serve You with a loyal heart and with a
willing mind; for You search all hearts and
understand all the intent of the thoughts. If
she seeks You, You will be found by her; but

if she forsakes You, You will cast her off
forever.

1 CHRONICLES 28:9

---------- ♥ ----------

I pray that my wife has been delivered from
the law, having died to what she was held
by, so that she should serve in the newness
of the Spirit and not in the oldness of the
letter.

ROMANS 7:6

---------- ♥ ----------

I pray that my wife will serve You, LORD, with
gladness and come before Your presence
with singing. I pray that she will know that
You, LORD, are God and that it is You who
have made her, and not she herself.

PSALM 100:2–3

42

SICKNESS

Heavenly Father, in accordance with the perfection of Your word, I pray that You will heal my wife of her affliction and restore her to health. We need Your help, and I pray Your word for that important need to be met. It is in the powerful name of Jesus that I ask. Amen.

God, in accordance with Your Word...

I pray that You will heal my wife, O Lord, and she shall be healed. Save her and she shall be saved.

JEREMIAH 17:14

❤

I pray, God, that You will restore health to my wife and heal her wounds.

JEREMIAH 30:17

I pray that my wife will diligently heed Your voice, Lord God, and do what is right in Your sight and give ear to Your commandments and keep all Your statutes, and that You will put no diseases on her.

EXODUS 15:26

♥

I pray, O God, that Jesus was wounded for my wife's transgressions and was bruised for her iniquities and by His stripes she is healed.

ISAIAH 53:5

♥

I pray, God, that You heal all my wife's diseases and redeem her life from destruction.

PSALM 103:3–4

♥

I pray that Jesus Himself bore my wife's sins in His own body on the tree, and that she, having died to sin, might live for

righteousness—by whose stripes she was
healed.

1 PETER 2:24

———— ♥ ————

I pray that my wife may prosper in all things
and be in health, just as her soul prospers.

3 JOHN 1:2

———— ♥ ————

I pray, O God, that my wife remembers that
Jesus healed every sickness and every
disease among the people.

MATTHEW 9:35

———— ♥ ————

I pray, Jesus, that power goes out from You
and heals my wife.

LUKE 6:19

I pray, God, that You have sent Your word and healed my wife and delivered her from destruction.

PSALM 107:20

———— ♥ ————

I pray, God, that I am not worthy that You should come under my roof. But only speak a word, and my wife will be healed.

MATTHEW 8:8

———— ♥ ————

I pray that the prayer of faith will save my wife from her sickness and that You, Lord, will raise her up. And if she has committed sins, she will be forgiven.

JAMES 5:15

43

SPIRITUAL GROWTH

Lord Jesus, there is no more powerful prayer that I can pray than to pray the word of God directly from the pages of the Bible. That is what I now do as I pray for my wife's spiritual growth. I pray that as Your word says she will take heed to herself and keep herself in accordance with Your word. Thank You for honoring Your words. Amen.

God, in accordance with Your Word...

I pray that my wife will beware, lest there be in her an evil heart of unbelief in departing from the living God. I pray that I will exhort her daily, while it is called "Today," lest she be hardened through the deceitfulness of sin.

HEBREWS 3:12–13

I pray that my wife does not forget You, the LORD her God, by not keeping Your commandments, Your judgments, and Your statutes which You command her today. I pray that she shall remember the LORD her God, for it is You who give her power to get wealth.

DEUTERONOMY 8:11, 18

***

I pray that my wife has not forgotten the name of her God, or stretched out her hands to a foreign god. Would You, God, not search this out? For You know the secrets of the heart.

PSALM 44:20–21

***

I pray, God, that my wife will be watchful, and strengthen the things which remain, that are ready to die, for she has not found her works perfect before You.

REVELATION 3:2

I pray that my wife will take heed to herself, and diligently keep herself, lest she forget the things her eyes have seen, and lest they depart from her heart all the days of her life.

DEUTERONOMY 4:9

———— ♥ ————

I pray, God, that my wife returns to You, and You will return to her.

MALACHI 3:7

———— ♥ ————

I pray that my wife will look diligently lest she fall short of Your grace, God; and lest any root of bitterness spring up causing trouble, and by this she becomes defiled.

HEBREWS 12:15

———— ♥ ————

I pray that after my wife has escaped the pollutions of the world through the knowledge of her Lord and Savior Jesus Christ, that she not become entangled in them and overcome.

2 PETER 2:20

44

STRENGTH

God, I call upon You now to give my wife more strength than ever before. I pray Your word that You will increase her strength according to Your word. In Jesus' precious name I pray. Amen.

God, in accordance with Your Word...

I pray, God, that You give power to my wife, who is weak, and that You increase her strength.

ISAIAH 40:29

♥

I pray that my wife shall wait on You, LORD, and that she shall renew her strength. I pray that she shall mount up with wings like eagles, they she shall run and not be weary, and that she shall walk and not faint.

ISAIAH 40:31

I pray that my wife will fear not, for You are with her. I pray that she will be not dismayed, for You are her God. I pray that You will strengthen her and help her and that You will uphold her with Your righteous right hand.

ISAIAH 41:10

♥

I pray that You, LORD, are my wife's rock and her fortress and her deliverer; her God, her strength, in whom she will trust; her shield and the horn of her salvation, her stronghold. I pray that she will call upon You, LORD, who are worthy to be praised; so shall she be saved from her enemies.

PSALM 18:2–3

♥

I pray that You, LORD, are my wife's light and her salvation. Whom shall she fear?

PSALM 27:1

I pray, God, that You will strengthen my wife according to Your word.

PSALM 119:28

———— ♥ ————

I pray that my wife will be strengthened with all might, according to Your glorious power, God.

COLOSSIANS 1:11

———— ♥ ————

I pray that my wife can do all things through Christ who strengthens her.

PHILIPPIANS 4:13

———— ♥ ————

I pray that You, God, will grant my wife, according to the riches of Your glory, to be strengthened with might through Your Spirit.

EPHESIANS 3:16

I pray that my wife will be strong in You, Lord, and in the power of Your might. I pray that she will put on the whole armor of God, that she may be able to stand against the wiles of the devil. For she does not wrestle against flesh and blood, but against principalities, against powers, against the rulers of the darkness of this age, against spiritual hosts of wickedness in the heavenly places.

EPHESIANS 6:10–12

♥

I pray that my wife will take up Your whole armor, God, that she may be able to withstand in the evil day, and having done all, to stand. I pray that she will stand therefore, having girded her waist with truth, having put on the breastplate of righteousness, and having shod her feet with the preparation of the gospel of peace; above all, taking the shield of faith with which she will be able to quench all the fiery darts of the wicked one. I pray also that she will

take the helmet of salvation, and the sword
of the Spirit, which is the word of God,
praying always with all prayer and
supplication in the Spirit.

EPHESIANS 6:13–18

45

TEMPTED

Jesus, Your word says that You know how to deliver my wife out of temptations. I pray right now that You will now and forevermore deliver the wife that I love so much from any temptation that she may encounter. I pray Your word for her in this area, and I trust You to do as Your word promises. In Your name I pray. Amen.

God, in accordance with Your Word...

I pray that You, Lord, know how to deliver my wife out of temptations.

2 PETER 2:9

— ♥ —

I pray that sin shall not have dominion over my wife, for she is not under law but under grace.

ROMANS 6:14

I pray, Lord, that Your word my wife has hidden in her heart, that she might not sin against You!

PSALM 119:11

♥

I pray that if my wife confesses and forsakes her sins she will have mercy.

PROVERBS 28:13

♥

I pray that if my wife confesses her sins, You are faithful and just to forgive her her sins and to cleanse her from all unrighteousness.

1 JOHN 1:9

♥

I pray, Lord, that my wife will not say when she is tempted, "I am tempted by God"; for You cannot be tempted by evil, nor do You Yourself tempt anyone. For she is tempted when she is drawn away by her own desires and enticed. Then, when desire has conceived, it gives birth to sin; and sin, when it is full-grown, brings forth death. I pray that my wife will not be deceived.

JAMES 1:13–15

———— ♥ ————

I pray that no temptation has overtaken my wife except such as is common to man; but You, God, are faithful, and will not allow her to be tempted beyond what she is able, but with the temptation You will also make the way of escape, that she may be able to bear it.

1 CORINTHIANS 10:13

———— ♥ ————

I pray that my wife does not have a High Priest who cannot sympathize with her weaknesses, but was in all points tempted as she is, yet without sin. Let her therefore come boldly to the throne of grace, that she may obtain mercy and find grace to help in time of need.

HEBREWS 4:15–16

I pray, Jesus, that You are able to aid my wife who is tempted.

HEBREWS 2:18

———— ♥ ————

I pray that my wife will be sober and vigilant; because her adversary the devil walks about like a roaring lion, seeking whom he may devour. I pray that she will resist him, steadfast in the faith, knowing that the same sufferings are experienced by her Christian brothers in the world.

1 PETER 5:8–9

———— ♥ ————

I pray that my wife will be strong in You, Lord, and in the power of Your might. I pray that she will put on Your whole armor, God, that she may be able to stand against the wiles of the devil, and that above all, she takes the shield of faith with which she will be able to quench all the fiery darts of the wicked one.

EPHESIANS 6:10–11, 16

I pray, God, that my wife will resist the devil
and that he will flee from her.

JAMES 4:7

———— ♥ ————

I pray, God, that He who is in my wife is
greater than he who is in the world.

1 JOHN 4:4

———— ♥ ————

I pray, Lord, that my wife will count it all
joy when she falls into various trials,
knowing that the testing of her faith produces
patience. I pray that blessed is my wife who
endures temptation; for when she has been
approved, she will receive the crown of life
which You have promised to those who
love You.

JAMES 1:2–3, 12

———— ♥ ————

I pray that You, God, are able to keep my
wife from stumbling and to present her

faultless before the presence of Your glory
with exceeding joy.

JUDE 1:24

———— ♥ ————

I pray that in this my wife will greatly rejoice,
though now for a little while, if need be, she
has been grieved by various trials, that the
genuineness of her faith, being much more
precious than gold that perishes, though it
is tested by fire, may be found to praise,
honor, and glory at the revelation of Jesus
Christ.

1 PETER 1:6–7

46

TROUBLES

~

Lord, Your word says that You will allow no more troubles than my wife can bear. Please honor Your word in my prayers, and take care of and strengthen my wife. It is in the authority of the name of Jesus that I pray. Amen.

God, in accordance with Your Word...

I pray that my wife shall obtain joy and gladness and that sorrow and sighing shall flee away.

ISAIAH 51:11

———— ♥ ————

I pray that my wife will be anxious for nothing, but in everything by prayer and supplication, with thanksgiving, will let her requests be made known to You, God, and Your peace, which surpasses all

understanding, will guard her heart and
mind through Christ Jesus.

PHILIPPIANS 4:6–7

♥

I pray, God, that You will comfort my wife
in all her tribulation, that she may be able
to comfort those who are in any trouble,
with the comfort with which she herself is
comforted by You.

2 CORINTHIANS 1:4

♥

I pray, God, that my wife does not worry
about tomorrow, for tomorrow will worry
about its own things.

MATTHEW 6:34

♥

I pray that all things work together for good
to my wife who loves You, God, to she who
is called according to Your purpose.

ROMANS 8:28

I pray that my wife will be glad and rejoice
in Your mercy, God, for You have considered
her trouble. You have known her soul in
adversities, and have not shut her up into
the hand of the enemy; You have set her
feet in a wide place.

PSALM 31:7–8

I pray that my wife's help comes from You,
LORD, who made heaven and earth.

PSALM 121:2

I pray that my wife will come boldly to the
throne of grace, that she may obtain mercy
and find grace to help her in time of need.

HEBREWS 4:16

I pray, God, that my wife will cast all her
care upon You, for You care for her.

1 PETER 5:7

I pray, O God, that my wife always
remembers that You are good, a stronghold
in her day of trouble; and that You know
that she trusts in You.

NAHUM 1:7

♥

I pray that though my wife is hard pressed
on every side, she is not crushed; she is
perplexed, but not in despair; persecuted,
but not forsaken; struck down, but not
destroyed.

2 CORINTHIANS 4:8–9

♥

I pray that though my wife walks in the midst
of trouble, You, God, will revive her. You
will stretch out Your hand against the wrath
of her enemies, and Your right hand will save
her.

PSALM 138:7

I pray that my wife will not let her heart be troubled. I pray that she believes in You, God, and also in Jesus.

JOHN 14:1

♥

I pray, God, that when my wife passes through the waters, You will be with her. And through the rivers, they shall not overflow her. When she walks through the fire, she shall not be burned, nor shall the flame scorch her. For You are the Lord her God.

ISAIAH 43:2–3

47

WAITING ON GOD

Heavenly Father, I really do believe that the most important thing that I can do is to pray Your very words and thoughts over my wife. Hear my prayers, and help my wife to wait on You. I pray everything in Jesus' wonderful name. Amen.

God, in accordance with Your Word...

I pray, God, that my wife will say in that day: "Behold, this is my God. I have waited for Him, and He will save me. This is the LORD; I have waited for Him. I will be glad and rejoice in His salvation."

ISAIAH 25:9

———— ♥ ————

I pray that my wife has become a partaker of Christ if she holds the beginning of her confidence steadfast to the end.

HEBREWS 3:14

I pray that my wife waits for You, LORD, that her soul waits, and in Your word she does hope.

PSALM 130:5

♥

I pray that my wife will wait on You, LORD, and that she will be of good courage. I pray also that You will strengthen her heart.

PSALM 27:14

♥

I pray, God, that my wife's soul waits silently for You alone and that her expectation is from You.

PSALM 62:5

♥

I pray, O God, that my wife will hold fast the confession of her hope without wavering, for You who promised are faithful.

HEBREWS 10:23

I pray that my wife shall wait on You, LORD, and that she shall renew her strength. I pray also that she shall mount up with wings like eagles and that she shall run and not be weary and walk and not faint.

ISAIAH 40:31

♥

I pray that my wife's soul waits for You, LORD, that You are her help and her shield.

PSALM 33:20

48

WORRIED

Most Precious God, I pray Your very words over the worries of my wife. You have promised to not let her heart be troubled if she will cast her cares on You. I pray that all worry will flee from her and that her joy will return. All of my prayers I pray in Jesus' name. Amen.

God, in accordance with Your Word...

I pray, God, that my wife will not let her heart be troubled.

JOHN 14:1

———— ♥ ————

I pray that my wife will cast all her cares upon You, God, for You care for her.

1 PETER 5:7

I pray that my wife will lie down in peace, and sleep; for You alone, O Lord, make her dwell in safety.

PSALM 4:8

———— ♥ ————

I pray that You, God, will keep my wife in perfect peace, she whose mind is stayed on You, because she trusts in You.

ISAIAH 26:3

———— ♥ ————

I pray, God, that my wife will let Your peace rule in her heart.

COLOSSIANS 3:15

———— ♥ ————

I pray that my wife will be anxious for nothing, but in everything by prayer and supplication, with thanksgiving, will let her requests be made known to You, God; and Your peace, which surpasses all

understanding, will guard her heart and
mind through Christ Jesus.

PHILIPPIANS 4:6–7

———— ♥ ————

I pray, God, that You shall supply all my wife's
needs according to Your riches in glory by
Christ Jesus.

PHILIPPIANS 4:19

———— ♥ ————

I pray that my wife will not worry about her
life, what she will eat or what her will drink;
nor about her body, what she will put on. I
pray that she will seek first Your kingdom,
God, and Your righteousness, and all these
things shall be added to her.

MATTHEW 6:25, 33

———— ♥ ————

I pray, Lord, that when my wife lies down,
she will not be afraid. I pray that she will
lie down and her sleep will be sweet.

PROVERBS 3:24

I pray that my wife will say of You, LORD,
"He is my refuge and my fortress; my God,
in Him I will trust."

PSALM 91:2

———— ♥ ————

I pray, O God, that great peace has my wife
who loves Your law, and nothing causes her
to stumble.

PSALM 119:165

———— ♥ ————

I pray, Jesus, that Your peace You leave with
my wife and that Your peace You give to
her; not as the world gives do You give to
her. Let not her heart be troubled, neither
let it be afraid.

JOHN 14:27

Seminars conducted by Lee Roberts include *Praying God's Will*, *Avoiding Failure in Your Christian Walk*, and *The Businessman, the Salesman, and God!*

More information on these seminars can be obtained by writing Lee Roberts, P.O. Box 671465, Marietta, GA 30067-0025, or by calling 404-956-8550.